PENGUIN BOOKS

THE IRISH

Sean O'Faolain was born in 1900 and educated at the
National University of Ireland. For a year he was a commercial traveller for books but gave it up to fight on the
side of De Valera in 1921. He was a member of the Irish
Republican Army for six years, taught for a further year
and then studied for three years at Harvard University.
For four years he taught at Strawberry Hill Training
College for Teachers, after which he turned to writing
and went back to his native Ireland, where he now lives
in Dublin. He has written some twenty books, including
travel and literary criticism, novels, biographies, and
several books of short stories. He has also contributed to
all the well-known periodicals in Great Britain and the
United States. His more recent publications are an autobiography, *Vive Moi!*, and the books of stories, *The Heat
of the Sun*, *The Talking Trees*, *Foreign Affairs and
other stories* and *And Again?* Sean O'Faolain is a D.Litt.
of Trinity College, Dublin. He is married, with two
children. His wife has written several books of Irish
folk-tales and his daughter Julia is also a writer.

Sean O'Faolain

THE IRISH

PENGUIN BOOKS

Penguin Books Ltd, Harmondsworth, Middlesex, England
Viking Penguin Inc., 40 West 23rd Street, New York, New York 10010, U.S.A.
Penguin Books Australia Ltd, Ringwood, Victoria, Australia
Penguin Books Canada Ltd, 2801 John Street, Markham, Ontario, Canada L3R 1B4
Penguin Books (N.Z.) Ltd, 182–190 Wairau Road, Auckland 10, New Zealand

—

First published in Pelican Books 1947
Revised edition 1969
Reprinted 1972
Reprinted in Penguin Books with a revised Appendix 1980
Reprinted 1981, 1984

—

—

Made and printed in Great Britain by
Hazell Watson & Viney Limited,
Member of the BPCC Group,
Aylesbury, Bucks
Set in Intertype Granjon

Thanks are due to Mrs W. B. Yeats and to Messrs Macmillan & Co. Ltd for permission to include the late W. B. Yeats' poem *The Unappeasable Host* (p. 29) from the *Collected Poems of W. B. Yeats;* and to Mr Padraic Colum for the use of his poem *I Shall Not Die for Thee* (p. 67).

*'History proper is the history of thought.
There are no mere events in history.'*

R. G. COLLINGWOOD

CONTENTS

EXPLANATION

THIS book is not a history of political events, although some political events are described briefly in the course of the main narrative. It is, in effect, a creative history of the growth of a racial mind; or one might call it a psychological history; or, if the term were not far too large and grandiose, the story of the development of a national civilization; although what has happened to the Irish mind is not an undisturbed local expansion but a complex process of assimilation at the end of which Ireland enters, with her own distinctive qualifications, into the great general stream of European culture.

Irish readers will have become so accustomed to another approach – the nationalist concept, almost wholly a political concept, of Ireland always on the defensive against foreign enemies – that they especially might, without this preliminary explanation, be a little taken aback at a record which looks at Nationality solely from the viewpoint of Civilization; which, for example, is interested almost exclusively in the great gifts brought to Ireland by the Norman invasion; which sees in the impact of all foreign influences not a political or even a military battleground but the battleground of a racial mind forced on each new occasion to struggle afresh with itself. Indeed, if this little book were not intended for the widest audience I might have dispensed with politics and war entirely, or merely referred without details, and in passing, to such tiresome events as invasions, reigns, parliaments, the rise and fall of dynasties, all of which can have no interest for anybody apart from what they contribute – generally without knowing it – to the sum of human civilization.

A word of self-excuse. Books like Trevelyan's *English Social History* are unknown for Ireland. Most histories are nationalist, patriotic, political, sentimental. I had not a single book to turn to which is not either preoccupied with the national ego and a delusion of its self-sufficiency, or else a cursive record of political events, or a source-book of these events. I know only two books on Irish history – apart, of course, from specialized scholarly works – that hack a clear perspective through the tangled jungles of futile and pointless raids, counter-raids, battles, sieges, 'victories' (over what is never otherwise made clear), and so forth: those are Edmund Curtis's one-volume *History of Ireland*, and Bishop Mathew's *The Celtic Peoples and Renaissance Europe*. These are highly civilized books. I have made acknowledgement, here and there in the text, to one or two special studies that have also seen the local story in a larger perspective. But, otherwise, this inadequate attempt at the interpretation of the Irish mind in labour has had to be, in its small and – nobody knows better than I – inadequate way, a pioneering effort, a hit or miss affair of instinct rather than knowledge. Some day somebody may write an 'Irish Social History' and give a quite different value to events.

In one place I have used the image of the signpost when speaking of an historical event, saying that it points forward to a modern development. That will at once reveal the weakness of all such essays as this. How do I know what the inscription on each signpost is? Only by looking back at it from the modern destination. But how do I know what this modern destination is? It is all very well for me to say – 'There you can see Irishmen at a milestone in their journey to what they have become today'. Who am I to say what the Irish mind is like today? I can say, 'Circumspice'. But one has only to be in Ireland for two days to know that the most popular Irish entertainment is to circumspect, and to disagree. The validity, then, of this book is largely a matter of its persuasiveness and credibility. There will always be a variety of historical explanations for modern achievements and failures (in themselves interchangeable words according to points of view). As the late R. G. Collingwood would have said, the truth of the answers will depend always on the questions which one asks. I hope I am at least clear as to my paramount question. Which is, to ask at every stage, 'What has this event or this contributed – with whatever racial colouring is no matter – to the sum of world-civilization?' Where I could see nothing of that nature emerge it seemed to me that the event was barren and I ignored it. Since, for these reasons, this little sketch ignores most of the incidents which are emphasized in our history books, and is, indeed, concerned not with incidents but with intelligence, it will seem to some far too simple a story. History, however, is often simpler than the historians make it.

In the first section I describe the raw material of the Irish nature or 'genius'; in the second, how intelligence begins to burgeon under stress; in the third, the six representative types which have branched from these origins – the peasantry, the Anglo-Irish, the rebels, the priests, the writers, and the politicians. There is another type which I have barely hinted at, the new middle classes, or native bourgeoisie; they are the peasant in process of development or final decay, it is too soon to say which.

PART I: THE ROOTS

PREHISTORY AND EARLY HISTORY *c.* 700 B.C. TO *c.* A.D. 500

Prehistoric Ireland, about 7000 B.C. *onward. The Stone Age begins.*

The Bronze Age: middle date, c. 1500 B.C. *The Iron Age, around* 500 B.C.

The Celts invade Ireland. The period dealt with in the great imaginative histories and romances.

Establishment of local states, and the beginning of regionalism or particularism.

The arrival of Christianity (fourth century) and beginnings of monasticism.

The development of the social system described in the 'Brehon Laws'.

WHO WERE THE CELTS?

A CAMERA-CARRYING satellite orbiting westward from Europe would now show, on the rim of the continent, a ragged-edged piece of land broken off the continental mass, ready at any moment to slide down the spherical waste of the Atlantic. It is an island of medium size as islands go, about four times larger than Sicily or Sardinia, somewhat smaller than Iceland or Cuba. Geographers and archaeologists have established that it was once attached to its neighbouring island; that both were once part of the continental landmass; and that it was not inhabited before 6000 B.C., when at the close of the post-glacial period the melting of the ice over northern Europe created a climate bearable by, if not exactly benevolent to man, animals and plants.

Its first nameless explorers, and ultimately nameless inhabitants, must have reached it by means of a land bridge at a time before the present Irish Sea existed. They probably first came as hunters and later established settlements – these could have been no more than the rudest shelters – on the tops of little hillocks in the north of the island, now known as *drumlins*, glacial deposits to be found all across the country from modern Antrim westward to modern Sligo. Further south similar deposits on ridges became known as *eiscirs*. One such, which became historically known as the *Eiscir Riada*, wanders across the middle of the island followed, in part, by the present road from Dublin to Galway. Remains of some of these primeval settlements may still be seen at Larne in County Antrim.

Once the ice finally melted and the level of the surrounding sea rose, Ireland – to give it its present name – became completely detached from Britain, the climate improved, the settlers were in some condition to master their environment and so we get the first permanent inhabitants of this most westerly island of Europe. We know almost nothing about them. We can only draw inferences. As their stone-age tools improved they would have planted corn and ground it in stone querns. They presumably bred some domestic animals, learned how to make some sort of pottery, and build some sort of houses. The remains of some houses of this early period have been excavated, in places like Lough Gur in County Limerick, and they indicate foundations of dry stones, with walls of woven wickerwork between wooden posts supporting thatched roofs. One or more of those huts would have been enclosed by an earthen rampart to shelter men and animals from the elements and wild beasts. By degrees these settlers must have learned how to make boats, and so begun to trade with and learn from places farther advanced in techniques, such as the Iberian peninsula to the southwest.

There, if they did not discover it for themselves, they would, for example, have learned about copper and its uses – there was, in fact, copper in plenty in the southern part of the island – and there, or elsewhere, or at home, they would have learned that when copper is mixed with tin it becomes harder and retains its cutting edge. The effect, in sum, was that the population increased in the copper-bearing south – there is no copper in the north – and found itself launched into what we would now call a new cultural and economic expansion. When gold and silver were also mined we get those famous Bronze Age gold ornaments now preserved in the National Museum in Dublin – gorgets, torcs or crescent-shaped lunulae decorated with delicate designs in circles and chevrons.

Most of these finds have been turned up accidentally by turf-cutters, ploughmen or labourers casually digging with the spade. The largest and most startling of these finds came to light in 1854 when a gang of labourers were cutting away the side of a small hill in Mooghane, in County Clare, to lay down the West Clare Railway. One of these men, with a single stroke of a pick, found a stream of gorgets, torcs and fibulae pouring out at his feet. He and his companions immediately started to fill their hats with the gleaming objects, and ran with them into the nearest village, Newmarket-on-Fergus, hard by the present Shannon Airport, where they exchanged immeasurable wealth for tea, sugar and oatmeal. It completes the picture of the vasty past into which these men had sunk their ignorant picks to say that on top of that little hill there is a large stone fort – close on four thousand years old – whose inhabitants, possibly faced by a sudden invasion, had buried all this wealth a few feet underground. This fort has three great circular stone walls, of which the outer wall, oval in shape, encloses some fifteen hundred feet by a thousand feet. The walls, of loose stone, are about fifteen feet thick. Other prehistoric forts are to be seen in Staigue, in County Kerry; on the cliff-edge over the sea on the largest of the Aran Islands; at Grianan Ailech in County Donegal.

Facing, as they do, centuries from which not a single document of the smallest kind remains, the archaeologists and historians have always had a special interest in the way prehistoric men buried their dead. In Ireland they followed the fashion then current along the Mediterranean and the Atlantic, from Iberia to Brittany, Britain, Scotland and around to Norway. They cremated their dead and either buried the remains, bones and ashes, in urns under great stones, or *dolmens*; or they placed them with a number of other cists, or funeral caskets, in a Passage Grave, or a Gallery Grave, on top of which they raised enormous tumuli of earth and stone. Today these tombs are to be seen at their most impressive some twenty-five miles north of Dublin, where a stone-age city of the dead extends for about a mile and a half on a ridge north of the River Boyne, about five miles inland from the little port of Drogheda. There are several of these great mounds, of which the best known are Knowth, Dowth and New Grange, perched high to command the ancient plain of Bregia, a wide area some of which these stone-age men may have painfully cleared with their stone-age axes to reveal the makings of the best grassland in Europe.

Even today it is an impressively rich plain, but in those early centuries when there was nothing at all to see on its far-spreading greenery but slowly moving clouds of flocks and herds it must have made a profound impression on the traveller coming on it out of the wellnigh impassable forests and thickets that covered so much of the rest of the island. But what some such early traveller may have felt on seeing the great tumuli rising against the sky we cannot even imagine; especially when, from a distance, he first saw the three main tumuli, about a mile apart from one another, grouped like clouds against the clouds – for they were not then as now, worn, green domes: they were outlined by walls of gleaming cloud-white basalt, and on each peak there stood a tall stone like a spike on a helmet.

The most rewarding of these remains of pre-Celtic Ireland is the tumulus now called New Grange. It is about 280 feet in diameter. Around its base there is a number of protective stones, originally a kerb for the mound itself. At the low entrance there is a highly-decorated slab, one of the best examples of its kind in the whole necropolis, described by one archaeologist as the most famous stone in the whole repertory of European megalithic art. Within the tumulus one finds more slabs carved with designs of lozenges, chevrons, spirals and concentric circles. The stone basins on the earthen floor were possibly used for cremation, but we find no urns now; New Grange was raided by the Danes in the tenth century and the urns were doubtless destroyed at that time. Since one of the roof stones has revealed more carvings on its back – evidently intended to be hidden from the eyes of men for all time – we can only feel that all these carvings were not just decorations but part of some religious or magical ritual whose significance we are now likely never to understand. As we look we feel in the presence of a lost world. We are out of touch. We have no bridge on which to step across so many centuries. It is as if our minds had lost a dimension in the darkness of an interrupted civilization.

It is not until about 300 B.C. that the fog lifts. We then find that the inhabitants of this island are, or include a people, who, in common with other similar peoples then occupying large areas of central Europe, speak a Celtic language, and in other ways resemble those continentals in their manner of life and social framework. Some historians and archaeologists put the date for the coming of the Celts as far back as 900 B.C. Some even venture to propose that the nameless people before these known Celts are also of Celtic origin, but this is pure speculation and it is always prefaced by a cautious 'It may be ...', or, a 'Some think ...' All that is certain is that the Celts were late invaders, that they brought their language and culture with them from Europe, and imposed them so thoroughly on the people they found in possession that not a scrap of tradition remains from those earlier inhabitants, nor even a word of their language: all that we have, to record them, are the physical remnants of their life-ways, forts, houses, rude tools, and elaborate burial rites. We know also that Ireland has ever since been so fundamentally Celtic that the language still spoken in those remote parts of the west, where it has never died, is the modern form of the Gaelic, or Goidelic, of the last wave of Celts, known as Goidels, who came here around the first century B.C.

To understand the subsequent development of the Irish mind it is essential to grasp at the start that the Celts were never a political nation. In Europe they had always lived in loosely-joined communities, without any political sense of cohesion between one community and the next, fatally lacking in that power to unite firmly, and stick together persistently, which distinguished the Romans, whose farthest-flung outposts in Britain or Iberia always looked to and were governed from their imperial capital. This individualism of the Celts was to continue in Ireland for many centuries, in parts as late as the sixteenth century, and it is a key to many of Ireland's later political weaknesses. Even when the Celts did settle down regionally their ancestral memory was essentially that of nomads, much given to moving, changing, and raiding, a pastoral rather than an agricultural people, so that it is no wonder that the central Irish saga, which stems from a queen's ambition to possess the finest and biggest bull in the country, is called the *Tain Bo Cuailgne*, or *The Cattle Raid of Cuailgne*.

The European Celts were, however, far from being a barbarian people; they had a culture of their own strong enough to exercise at least some influence on the early Germanic peoples. When Rome finally conquered Gaul and introduced Latin learning there it was the old Celtic schools of the druids who took over the teaching of classical culture, so successfully that within a few generations Latin language and Latin learning were widely disseminated in that part of the Empire. They were reckless fighters – they often fought stark naked. They sacked Rome in 387 B.C. Others, spreading across the Balkans, were powerful enough to make a treaty with Alexander the

Great. When St Paul wrote his Epistle to the Galatians he was addressing people of Celtic origin. They were skilled metal workers. That their leaders were often rich, race-proud and aristocratic-minded we may infer from the manner in which in Europe they buried their noble dead, with their choicest arms and weapons, or their highly carved and decorated chariots. They had probably reached the highest point of their culture around 500 B.C. – the round date for their famous decorative art now called La Tène, after the site on Lake Neuchâtel where it is supposed to have originated.

Driven to the ultimate west by the pressures of other groups it was these men who ultimately found living room in Ireland, if not exactly a *quieta patria*. They had to fight to establish themselves; and they went on fighting among themselves for group power in a pattern of internecine war that was to end only with the final English conquest of Ireland. For in Ireland they lived, much as the Celts of the continent must have lived, in groups or small 'states' called *tuatha*, each with its own chief or 'king'; each of which could, from time to time, fall under the domination of a more powerful neighbour. At any time a group could, by accretion, become dynastically powerful and even establish a shaky form of control over the whole country. But there never was at any time a centralized political system, or High Kingship, in Ireland. Indeed, not until the fifth century A.D. do we get any even moderately reliable information about such a High King, one Loegaire (anglicé Leary), whose rise to power is dated 428 A.D. and who died in 463 A.D.

Partly because of, and partly in spite of these dynastic struggles for power a fairly tight-looking social system gradually began to emerge. There were free and unfree, or independent and vassal statelets or *tuatha*. A stratified class-system seems to have become established, ranging downward from king to noble, poet, man of learning, druid, genealogist, tenant, crafts-man, horseman, landless men, outlaws, strangers, on down to the helot or virtual slave who had no rights or protection inside the laws, all duly mapped out (clearly but theoretically) and (also theoretically) leaving no room for dispute. But all such laws were, in practice, inevitably subject to the relativism and determinism of that constant struggle of the more powerful to get still more power, and of the less powerful to evade subjection or exploitation.

It is in the light of all this that we read the early epic literature of these people. Read superficially much of it is, indeed, all about the desire of Queen Maeve of Connaught (in the West) to gain possession of the superlatively splendid Brown Bull of Cuailgne (in the North). Read less superficially it seems to be a symbolic reflection of a dynastic struggle between western and northern power. But as the west had been settled from the south-east, symbolized by Tara, we have to change the centres of this dynastic struggle accordingly. It is all, furthermore, so shot through by the imaginative transformation of military fact into epic fancy that we may well doubt if Queen Maeve ever even existed, and may think of her, rather, as an early goddess turned, for epic purposes, into a human being. The whole of this central epic, indeed, is so blown out by Celtic wonder and imagination, so filled with attendant supernatural powers, gods and goddesses who replace, as they glorify, what had once been actual fighting men, that none of it can possibly be taken literally. Irish literature may, like the Greek epics, reflect remote historical facts. Like them, it supplies none. Its value and its delight is the light it throws on the Irish mind, on the early constituents of the Irish dye.

2

THE GREAT GODS DIE

If we turn to this early Irish literature, as we naturally may, to see what sort of people the Irish were in the infancy of the race, we find ourselves instead wandering in delighted bewilderment through a darkness shot with lightning and purple flame. One expects the beginnings of any people to be dark; the darkness at the beginning of the story of the Irish mind is an unnatural darkness. There is somewhat too much of the supernatural about it. Alternatively we may feel that here a racial imagination has, from the start, got out of control; or we may simply say that early Irish literature is wildly romantic; or that the popular idea of the Celt as a romantic is correct; or that the nineteenth century, in exploiting this romantic quality, committed only the fault of piling on top of something already sufficiently embroidered by nature a lot of superfluous William Morris trappings. But the impression of a supernatural infusion is, I think, far and away the most important one.

The Celt's sense of the Otherworld dominated his imagination and affected his literature from the beginning. So I see him, at any rate, struggling, through century after century, with this imaginative domination, seeking for a synthesis between dream and reality, aspiration and experience, a shrewd knowledge of the world and a strange reluctance to cope with it, and tending always to find the balance not in an intellectual synthesis but in the rhythm of a perpetual emotional oscillation.

This is to anticipate, and in this book I shall oscillate a great deal myself between the past and the present, ringing one against the other, which is the disadvantage as well as the only way of writing the psychological history of a people. For the moment I must presume that my reader will have some knowledge of early Celtic literature. The great tales must be well known, Deirdre and Conchubar, Cuchulainn and Emer and Fand and Etain, Diarmuid and Grainne, Oisin and Fionn. The modern romantic poets who have made them popular have sinned only in softening their starkness and decorating their decoration. But the gods do whistle in the air, appear and vanish, hover, shimmer through a veil, the Otherworld is always at one's shoulder and the sense of poetry is everywhere, though not always tamed to its purpose and never, outside the lyrics to which we must return later, winnowed of its chaff.

I will mention, very briefly, one run from one example to remind the reader of the highly imaginative quality of Celtic invention – the end of the piece called 'The Second Battle of Mag Tured' from the history book called *The Book of Invasions*. It depicts the end of the war between the (imaginary) peoples known as the Tuatha De Danaan and the Fomorians, who held them in bondage. It begins with the entry into the subject Nuada's palace at Tara, of a warrior called Lug Lamfada, or Lugh of the Long Arm, whose prowess is so great that Nuada considers how to use him against the Fomorians. The passage which follows lifts us at once out of the world of history:

Thereafter the wizards of Ireland were summoned to them and their medical men and charioteers and smiths and farmers and lawyers. They held speech with them in secret. Then Nuada inquired of the sorcerer whose name was Mathgen what power he could wield. He answered that through his contrivance he could cast the mountains of Ireland on the Fomorians, and roll their summits against the ground. And he declared to them that the twelve chief mountains of the land of Erin would support the Tuatha De Danaan, to wit, Slieve League and Denna Ulad and the Mourne Mountains, and Bri Ruri and Slieve Bladma and Slieve Snechta and Slieve Mish and Nefin and Slieve Maccu Belgadan and Segais and Cruachain Aigle ...

And the lochs of Ireland would dry before them and all the great rivers, but the Tuatha should drink as they needed. Then we hear of the Dagda, and Ogma, and the three gods of the Danaan people, and a plethora of themes enters with more magical servants, on both sides, including the Fomorian demigod, Balor of the Evil Eye:

An evil eye had Balor the Fomorian. That eye was never opened save on a battlefield. Four men used to lift up the lid of the eye with a polished handle which passed through its lid. If an army looked at that eye though they were many thousands in number, they could not resist a few warriors ...

But Lug, so soon as Balor's eye was opened, cast a sling-stone right through the eye, and that stone passed through Balor's head and killed twenty-seven Fomorians. Indeed, so many were slain in that battle that they could never be reckoned 'until we number the stars of heaven, sand of sea, flakes of snow, dew on lawn, hailstones, grass under feet of herds, and the horses of Manannan Mac Lir [the waves] in a storm at sea'.

As one reads these elaborations – in, I repeat, an alleged historical record – the mind cannot help being a little dazed. As we shall see presently there is one other paramount reason for this besides the immediate spectacle of imagination drowning in its own excess, or besides the natural difficulty of then-thinking into times so remote: that paramount reason being our comparative ignorance of the mythological, or religious, back references hidden in these heroic inventions.

But before we come to that we must advert to a further and purely mechanical reason for a sense of confused bewilderment. We do not read the literature as it was originally created. Later Christian scribes and patriotic pseudo-historians freely altered original records and traditional lore to suit their own ends, so that what we read today is a much-used palimpsest, and it is the delight and agony of modern scholars to try to peel off the second, third, fourth, and, for all we know, four-hundredth retelling in order to expose the original thought. Not that the original thought, if it ever could be discovered, would itself be firmly stated. The early Irish shaped their notions of this life, and the other life, at a stage in their development when they had passed far beyond savagery but had not yet arrived at civilization: that stage in human development when man's concepts are still fluid and formative, as well as when the arts of literature and design, which would have fixed the forms and attributes, for example, of their gods cannot keep pace with the imagination in labour. We Irish had no primitive Homer to shape our early, half-formed ideas into a connected whole, and the winds of time and latter-day piety have further blown these earliest dreams like smoke in wind about the sky. Myth and history, dreams and facts, are forever inextricably commingled.

It is therefore impossible to form any clear picture of the religious background of this primitive Ireland. Gods and demigods abound. The hierarchy is not to be codified. All one can say, and even that debatably and daringly, is that the great Jove of the Celts was the Dagda, which simply means the Good Father, also called the Oll-Athair or All Father, the god of the Otherworld, and that he was primarily a sungod; though, as one might expect from so mighty and central a deity, he had many functions and aspects and many names and many offshoots, or doublets, or imitators, or demigods born of his endlessly procreative plasma. Had Christianity not intervened it is likely, at least it is possible, that these recreations from the one great archetype and primitive myth would have developed characteristics and lives of their own, and the end might have been a coherent Celtic pantheon. As it is, the scholars, coming on these vaguely characterized creatures – part god, part hero, partly humanized, partly 'explained' – can only assume that *Aed Alainn* (The Lovely Aed), or *In Ruad Rofhessa* (The Red and All-wise One), or *Goll* (The One-eyed), and scores beside, are all born of the one adoration. It is even held that the name of Ireland, *Eriu,* modern Irish *Eire,* is that of a sungoddess.*

The attributes of the parent Dagda, Good Father, sungod, or Otherworld-god, are, at any rate, clearly consonant with sunworship. He is of enormous size; he rules the weather and the crops; he is swift; he wields a deadly club, which may be lightning; he owns a cauldron as inexhaustible as the cornucopia, and he is thought then to preside over the feasts of the Otherworld; he is very old and very wise, indeed he is the source of all wisdom, especially of occult wisdom. So must the Dagda have seemed, variously, as occasion suggested, to the early Irish.

Let us see an example of how time has treated these early gods. 'It was natural,' says Professor O'Rahilly, 'to atttribute great age and great knowledge to the deified sun, the heavenly eye who has observed the doings of countless ages of men.' It

* In all this section I obediently follow the most scholarly book on the subject – *Early Irish History and Mythology,* by Professor T. F. O'Rahilly, Institute of Advanced Studies, Dublin, 1946.

may be part of an early and simultaneous totemism that this sungod is thought able to assume the shape of animal or bird, such as the horse or the eagle who fly so swiftly and beautifully through the air. Elsewhere the animal who pre-eminently symbolizes the powers of the netherworld has been the serpent; but there are no serpents in Ireland and one alternative transformation of the sungod chosen by the Irish was the salmon. (This folk-practice of replacing any item which is not locally feasible by one which *is* locally feasible is widespread: e.g. in inland countries a folk-hero cannot descend into the sea but can descend a lake or a well, and some far-travelled story about him will, accordingly, be altered in this respect.) Now this Salmon of Knowledge is well known in Irish tales. They locate him, with due local patriotism, in various rivers, including the River Boyne, which is presided over by one of the various equivalents of the Dagda in human form, a hero named Elcmar. In an anecdote from the great Ulster, or Cuchulainn cycle, Cuchulainn – the central Irish hero – attempts to catch this Salmon of Wisdom and is opposed by Elcmar.

Therein the Celt is dualistically thinking of the gods as, at one and the same time, beneficent and maleficent. The gods possess wisdom, but the gods also guard their wisdom: to win it man must fight the gods. But it is not so stated – for the god is depicted as a human hero guarding his second self transformed into a salmon. The listeners to the tale would only partly perceive the divine truth behind the mortal tale. As time passed the mortal tale would come more and more into the foreground; the primitive belief would fade; in the end, the great gods would die.

Nevertheless, although rationalization, changes of nomenclature, euhemerization due to Christian distaste for the old beliefs, might actually improve the elementary myth, even alter it to great artistic advantage, behind the veil it is the elementary myth which still dominates and excites the imagination. We, however, having lost the primitive key to the primitive gate, must be content to read the tales purely as mortal tales. We may take them as shimmering reflections of the primitive Celtic mind, but we must not think of them as its pure creations. They are, rather, the recreations of the civilized Celt many many centuries after the passing into oblivion of the magnificently barbaric world which first set the wheel of wonder into movement.

There is a very pleasant example of the skill with which the Christian adaptors transformed the gods not merely into mortal heroes but into those new demigods – the saints. It occurs in Muirchus' *Life of Saint Patrick*. Here St Patrick thunders against sun-worship, declaring that all who adore the sungod will perish; but the Sun whom he worships shall endure for ever, and all who adore Him abide with Him forever. Patrick is opposed by one Coll, or Goll, meaning The One-eyed, which is a common image for the sun; later this Coll becomes Mac-Cuill, the Son of Coll, and gradually MacGuill, Maguil, and Machaldus. This man plans to murder Patrick. But Patrick by his own great miraculous power so astonishes his enemy that he becomes converted and, as a penance, Machaldus is set adrift in a rudderless and oarless coracle which bears him, ultimately, to the Isle of Man. There pious tradition made him into a Manx saint – St Maughold. It is a transformation of sun into saint which is not alone illustrative of the process by which pagan god becomes Christian hero but, also, of the infusion of pagan mythology into Christian hagiography. The early Irish mind is, apparently, as fertile when creating miracles as myths, though rarely as graceful. The imaginative dominance is not, at any rate, lessened by the arrival of Christianity.

We must see, too, how the historians worked their will on the gods. The most elaborate of their works is that great volume known as *The Book of Invasions*, a twelfth-century text, but doubtless begun several centuries earlier. The nineteenth-century scholars, such as Eugène O'Curry, took this volume as more or less genuine history; it is a measure of modern Irish scepticism that its latest critic roundly describes it as 'a deliberate work of fiction'. Its compilers set out to do several things: first, to explain, with considerable imaginative power, how it was that a variety of people seemed to have settled, from time to time, in this now supposedly purely 'Gaelic' island (those Goidels or Gaels who were the last wave of Celtic invaders); second, to unify the country politically by giving all the contemporary upper classes a common Gaelic origin; thirdly, they set out with 'the deliberate intention of reducing the faded deities of pagan Ireland to the status of mere mortals'.

One of the finest inventions of these pious frauds was one completely imaginary invasion by those folk whom we have already met in 'The Battle of Mag Tured' – the Tuatha De Danaan – the word *dán* apparently means artistic skill of any kind. Thereafter, if, for example, the people of the wild, mountainous south-west looked on the two great rounded hills against the horizon which, to this day, are called the Two Breasts of Danu, it was hoped that they would see in these mighty prostrate paps not some ossification of a monstrous heathen goddess but some fanciful image related to these (imaginary) mortal colonists. And all the gods and all the demigods would likewise be referred to this human origin, explained and demoted.

But though a racial imagination may be tamed or disciplined (and these redactions are primitive efforts to do this), it cannot be explained away into insensibility. If one could personify it one might imagine it saying obstinately, 'No, no! If to believe is sinful, to half-believe is but a fancy. We will not reason the gods out of existence. We will dream them into demigods and fancy them where they may live in immortal peace.' So, in the sagas the demigods abound, come and go, do not die but hide deep in the earth, in marvellous palaces known as *side* – pronounced *shee* – and if the curious asked later where these *shee* were, then men would point to the great burial mounds, such as Brugh na Boinne, those vast tumuli which may still awe the modern traveller at Knowth, Dowth and New Grange. Three of them have been opened and show great mortuary chambers, like that at New Grange, one of the largest in western Europe, now empty. (Even so did the Greeks attribute their prehistoric monuments to the Cyclops.) This word *side* became, still later, transferred from these 'palaces' to their occupants. In modern Gaelic it has come to mean what we call the fairies. And there, indeed, the great gods have at last died, not by being humanized but by being reduced to the status of elves, wood-nymphs, hobgoblins, brownies, local Lares, poor remnants of a great myth. In the nineteenth century to give any credence even to these displeased the clergy. The country folk talk of them nowadays hardly at all. They tend, I think, to speak only of what they call the *sprid*, the spirit, or ghost, a frightening and rather malevolent element; and, in any case, Irish 'fairy stories' as gathered from the people have never had much of the dainty or sparkling or pretty about them. Awe has remained to the end.

It was this mingled and confused memory that Yeats gathered into such poems as *The Unappeasable Host*:

> The Danaan children laugh, in cradles of wrought gold,
> And clap their hands together, and half-close their eyes,
> For they will ride the North when the ger-eagle flies
> With heavy whitening wings and a heart fallen cold;
> I kiss my wailing child and press it to my breast
> And hear the narrow graves calling my child and me.
> Desolate winds that cry over the wandering sea;
> Desolate winds that hover in the flaming West;
> Desolate winds that beat the doors of Heaven and beat
> The doors of Hell and blow there many a whimpering ghost;
> O heart the winds have shaken, the unappeasable host
> Is comelier than candles at Mother Mary's feet.

He kept various strands – the power of the Otherworld beings to carry off children and leave changelings in their place, their trick of appearing as birds or animals, their dwelling under the earth, their malevolence, their beauty. His poem is an interweaving of centuries upon centuries of bright imaginings and dim rememberings, of irrational terror and delight.

It was his immense good fortune to be born into an Ireland where that traditional memory still flourished, and so to see her as an ancient land, old as Judea and Egypt, with an ancient soul and an ancient aura, to find in her people a great dignity and a great simplicity and a great sense of wonder. Out of it all he created an aesthetic based on the instinctive life of the soul and the passionate life of the body as against such destructive things as cold character and sterile knowledge that generalizes all spontaneous life away into abstractions. He saw a folk-Ireland which is, even yet, far from dead though, like its beliefs, it now lives, as it were, underground. It takes three whiskeys to evoke it.

Our first approach to the early Irish world, through its

literature, is thus a bewilderment not only because of its own imaginative richness but because of a deliberate mingling of history, myth, legend and religion – possibly our ancestors' first effort to synthesize an imaginative concept of life with their actual experience of it. It may have been this mingling (though he may not have fully appreciated its disintegrating effects) that forced one of the most sensitive as well as intelligent British scholars who ever examined Irish literature, the late W. P. Ker, to assert that the Celt never could create an epic – his genius was for Romance. Epic, Ker defined as 'great actions in narrative with the persons well defined'; that is, tales marked by their weight and solidity rather than by their mystery and fantasy, tales of men striving for human ends by their own right hands, tales from which the ultimate emergence was their human dignity rather than the adventitious dignity of semi-divinity or semi-historicity. He goes on:

Many nations, instead of an *Iliad* or an *Odyssey*, have had to make shift with conventional repetitions in praise of chieftains, without any story; many (he is here referring to early Irish literature) have had to accept from their storytellers all sorts of monstrous adventures in place of the humanities of debate and argument. Epic literature is not common. . . . The growth of the true epic is a progress towards intellectual and imaginative freedom.

This interior struggle towards 'intellectual and imaginative freedom' goes on in every race. The struggle between the myth and the human drama is apparent even in the *Iliad* and the *Odyssey*, though Ker is surely right in saying that when, at the end of the *Odyssey*, silence falls on the listeners it is the silence of admiration for the narrator rather than wonder at his exploits. This is a matter of proportion. All wonder has gone out of such Saxon pieces as *The Fight at Maldon*; what remains is an eroded human interest. A choking superabundance of wonder dims the human figures in the Celtic sagas. The scribes who tried to humanize gods into credible heroes, were, in so far, moving towards intellectual freedom; when they turned them into incredible saints, they were moving backwards again into intellectual slavery; when the scribes were pseudo-historians they were, quite simply, selling their mythology for a mess of patriotic pottage. So, as we now have it, what pleases us most in the great central saga of *The Tain Bo Cuailgne*, or *The Driving Away of the Bull of Cooley*, are those rare runs in which definable characters do emerge, such as the curtain-lecture between Queen Maeve and her husband, or the unwilling fight between Cuchulainn and his dear boyhood friend Fer Diad.

This medley of myth and realism must have forged a strangely dual mind in the race that found itself oscillating so gently between both. Possibly the greatest degree of objectivity that the native mind can have reached when listening to these half-credible, half-incredible wonders – which, as with the folk of today or yesterday, was not just something adverted to occasionally and briefly but something impinging on them at every hour of their lives – was that of the old West Cork woman who was asked, 'Do you really believe in the fairies?' and who replied, 'I do not, but they're there!' It is irrelevant for the scholars, in their preoccupation with the origins of tales, to say that when mortals come and go, Orpheus-like, between this world and the Otherworld – as in the beautiful love-story of Midir and Etain – we are not to take this literally because these voyagers are, of course, former deities humanized by later redactors. In humanizing the gods the recreators simultaneously made their doings more natural, and more monstrous. They dilated the human imagination that had to cope with the half-divine immensely more than if they had left it wholly divine.

One feels, then, from the beginning of the Christian period, in the presence of a delightful dualism – moderns would call it split-mindedness – whenever one wanders into this early Irish world. There may be an overlay of stern Christian morality. At bottom there is a joyous pagan amorality. They believe in Hell. They also believe in the Happy Isles. They believe in the Christian doctrine of punishment or compensation in the afterlife. They believe, simultaneously, in the continuance of life's normal mortal joys and sorrows for all beyond the setting sun and behind the dripping udders of the clouds. With one lobe of their minds they live what Vendryes has called the life of a free independent and impetuous people, drunk on war and victory . . . [full of] the joy of adventure even in the land of fairies . . . a sense of marvel felt in the chronicles penned by the monks in the silence of the convent; for even in the holy legends and the lives of the saints one hears an echo of it, giving us a hagiography so different to that of the continent.

Another lobe of their minds, or is it the same lobe, shot-silk at the turn of a fold, a trick of the sun, must unseat their lusty human joy, their gay reliance, leaving them hung in mid-air between their various heavens and earths.

To sum up, the Celt never formulated a religion. The very extravagance with which his imagination peopled this life with glorious, half-mortal beings tells us that though he could sublimate this world he could not transcend it. His idea of Heaven is free of Time but it is rooted in Place. He never passed out of the animistic stage of belief in what we may call devils or angels, and Christianity was therefore easily able to push aside a paganism so sparse of thought that we may say it was without thought. Imagination alone cannot formulate a religion; it can scarcely even aspire to it. Something was, perhaps is, missing in the Celt of whose presence we are at once aware in the Greeks, the Hebrews and the Oriental peoples. Was it that they had an inadequate ethical sense? Was it that they loved life too well, so that one may think, for example, that the concept of the Fall of Man, the greatest contribution made by the Jews to modern religious thought, could never have come from a people so imaginatively in love with Man himself?

3

THE POETS' PICTURE

THE best old Irish poets are the anonymous lyrists, some Christian, mostly pagan, but all eloquent of that free and mobile life of which Vendryes speaks so affectionately. We will find the most attractive human pictures of that early Irish world, I suggest, not in the greater sagas but in these pre-tenth-century lyrics and the Middle Irish Ossianic tales and poems.

The constant motifs are the open air, the hunt, the changing seasons, love, animals, food and drink. That life seems very close to us, when, for example, Oisin, returning to earth after hundreds of years in the Land of the Young, finds his old pagan world gone and the new Hero reigning – Saint Patrick. He is listening to the saint, humbly and sadly, when, suddenly, he hears the blackbird's whistle. Lifting his hand he cries:

> The call of the blackbird of Derrycairn,
> The belling of the stag from Caill na gCaor,
> That is the music by which Finn met early sleep;
> And the wild duck of Loch na dTri Caol,
>
> The grouse in Cruachan Cuinn,
> The otter whistling in Druin da Loch,
> The eagle crying in Gleann na bFuath,
> The laughter of the cuckoo in Cnoc na Scoth;
>
> The dogs barking from Gleann Caoin
> The scream of the eagle from Cnoc na Sealg,
> The pattering of the dogs returning early
> From the Strand of the Red Stones . . .
>
> Ah! When Finn and the Fian lived
> They loved the mountain better than the monastery,
> Sweet to them the blackbird's call.
> They would have despised the tonguing of your bell!

We get the same intimate touch when this aged Oisin allows his 'poor bald pate' to be washed by a Christian woman and remembers the time when his hair was long and fine and fair, and how his teeth, now mere sunken rocks, 'would crunch the yellow-topped nuts'.

> They'd gnaw the haunch of a stag,
> Hard and hungry and hound-like;
> They'd not leave a jot or a joint
> That they would not mince.

Love and the chase are mingled in one of the sweetest of all these poems – Grainne's sleep-song for her lover Diarmuid one night when, worn out by their flight from their enemies, he falls asleep (so one imagines it) with his head in her lap and she, listening to the little noises all around from the disturbed animals in the darkness, knows their enemies must be near, but says, softly:

> Sleep a little, a little little longer,
> thou needst not feel or fear or dread,
> lad to whom I gave my love,
> son of O'Duibhne – Diarmuid . . .
>
> The stag is not asleep in the east,
> he never ceases belling,
> although he is cosy in the blackbirds' wood,
> he has no mind for sleeping.
>
> Why is not the hornless doe asleep,
> calling for her speckled calf?
> Running over the tops of the bushes
> she cannot sleep in her lair.
>
> The linnet is awake and twittering
> above the tips of the swaying trees:
> they are all chattering in the woods –
> even the thrush is not asleep.
>
> Why does not the wild duck sleep,
> not sleep, nor drowse?
> Why does it not sleep in its nest?
> Why is it swimming madly with all its strength?

Tonight the grouse is not asleep
above the high, stormy, heathery hills,
clear and sweet the cry of her throat,
sleepless among the streams.

Caoilte is loosed, O Diarmuid, on your track!
Caoilte's running will not take him astray.
Freed from death and dishonour
sleep in everlasting sleep. . . .

It is in these lyrics that one gets the clearest vignettes of that
free mobile life of the fern, before there ever was even a coastal
town in Ireland. Here pictures form clearly, freed from the ab-
struseness of contemporary or local mythical references now
hardly to be understood, like little snatches of landscape
through a mountain mist; as when Deirdre, taken away from
her lover Naoisi by the lustful old King Conchubar, remembers
sadly the happy days when she and Naoisi and his two brothers
lived in the mountains.

'Yes!' she says. 'You are proud of your soldiers, marching
into your palace after a foray, and think them a glorious sight.
But how lovely it was to see –

Naoisi brewing the mead from the sweet hazel nuts,
Or bathing with me beside the fire,
On Ardan with an ox or a fat hog,
Or Ainnle crossing the flooded river with faggots
        on his back.

'You think your pipers and your trumpeters make fine music?
But –

It was lovely when the voice of Naoisi
Rose like a wave,
Or Ardan stringing on his harp,
Or Ainnle humming as he went into his wild hut.'

Unlike the composers of the sagas these lyric poets are always
particularizing, as when one makes Deirdre recall the litany of
the glens of Scotland –

Glen Laid!
I used to sleep there under the white rocks.

Fish and flesh and rich badger
Was my share in Glen Laigh.

Glen Masain!
Tall its wild garlic, white its stalks.
We slept uneasily
Over the rough estuary of Masain.

Glen Eitchi!
There I raised my first house.
Delightful its wood, after rising.
A pen for the sun was Glen Eitchi.

Glen Da Ruadh!
Welcome every man who has a right to it,
Sweet is the cuckoo on the bending branch,
On the peak above Glen Da Ruadh.

Image after image clinches in a line some aspect of the season in their poems on winter and summer. Winter itself is in,

A river is each furrow on the slope.

All summer is in,

The sail gathers, perfect peace!

Or who needs to be told what season this is:

Blades of corn lie around cornfields
over the region of the brown world.

The feel of spring is in each line of:

The cold will spring up in one's face:
the ducks of the pool have raised a cry,
from wilderness wolf-packs scent
the early morning.

We know nothing about these poets, whether they were men or women, laymen or clerics, young or old – and yet I think one can tell safely that they were, whatever they professed to be, pure pagans. There is not the slightest trace of even a pantheistic belief in their Nature verse. Nature *was*, and nothing more: as in this random, and isolated quatrain:

> Cold the night in Moin Moir,
> A powerful rainstorm pours down.
> A wild tune – at which the clear wind laughs –
> is wailing over the shelter of the woods.

The poet turned with an equal vitality to almost everything that in his daily life he had to meet. That objectivity recompenses us for the mystery of his name. If we but let a little freedom to our sympathies we can feel back at his side in an instant, unsundered by strangeness in his beliefs or ours, at one with his delight, indifferent to his mask.

When he says, with the air of a man looking over a half-door, in another isolated scrap:

> A little bird
> Has let a piping from the tip
> Of his shining yellow beak –
> The blackbird from the yellow-leaved tree
> Has flung his whistle over Loch Laigh.

(and that, by the way, is all there is of it) we can surely feel the same physical delight, the same identical pleasure that he felt, and nothing to mar that pleasure but the withdrawal of our smile in thinking, with a melancholy that has nothing to do with the little poem, that bird, and tree, and whistle – and man – passed out of this world almost a thousand years ago.*

The synthesis is a personal one; the achievement is individual; but this will not be the only place in which the heart-beat of personal genius seems to be the best interpreter of a race.

---

* This quotation and the translations are from my anthology of old Irish poetry, *The Silver Branch*, Cape, London, 1937. Far better translations though less literal, occur in Frank O'Connor's *Kings, Lords and Commons*. The best translations of all, literal, scholarly, sensitive, are in Kuno Meyer's *Ancient Irish Poetry*.

4

THE SOCIAL REALITY

THE way of life that lies behind these romances was at once pastoral and warlike; that of a people who varied their modest agriculture and the tending of their vast herds by border wars to add to their wealth. They lived free, casual lives under the open sky inside (and the adjective is paramount) *local* horizons; which means that they remained, in dwindling enclaves of antiquity, up to the seventeenth century and the completion of the English conquest, a regionalist people who never developed a commercial sense, an elaborate husbandry, or a town life. The Danes and the Normans founded every Irish town that exists; the Tudors founded the rest. Dublin, Wexford, Wicklow, Limerick, Cork – all Danish. Kilkenny is a typical Norman creation. The Irish never founded a town. The finest thing they did in this way was the creation of monastic settlements, and these time scattered as the wind blows the ash of a burnt-out fire.*

No towns, then, unlike Roman Britain; no roads; only beaten paths, stony or muddy; very few buildings, an enclosed, possibly covered-over rath or earthen circle, bothies of clay and woven branches – for architecture, as we know it, comes only with Christianity in small, graceful churches of the type called Hiberno-Romanesque; everywhere dark and well-nigh impassable woods – battles in 'passes' generally meant passes through forests; a climate even more moist than in our time; vast stretches of uninhabited land; and everywhere the country's gold – herds of cattle; a great chieftain or 'king' might own a thousand cows. One may imagine how it was that the Danes could never

---

*Some students of Irish history argue that these monastic settlements, performing the function of universities, were 'towns'. The matter is easily disposed of. If Oxford contained nothing but a university it could not be called a town. Is Harvard a town? The only sensible definition of a town is its purpose and its legal rights: the former chiefly military or commercial; the latter the right to civil government.

penetrate far beyond the coast except along rivers for brief and daring raids inland, and that even the Normans could only drive wedges into the more passable valleys, and then always have inimical and unconquerable fastnesses on their flanks. The life-mode of such a land could defy the challenges of the outer world for a very long time: it actually persisted with an amazing toughness until the seventeenth century, so that in the heyday of Queen Elizabeth great parts of Ireland were still living much as their ancestors had lived in the days of Cuchulainn.

The leitmotif of Gaelic society from time immemorial had been the lowing of cattle. So persistent and dominant was that note in the lives of the generations, raised almost to the stature of a myth by the national epic, that the Bull might well have become the Bull God and some ingenious scholar may yet interpret the Dagda not as the Good Father, the Sun, but as the All Father, the Bull, to be adored as an emblem of fertility, a guarantee of a life that need never languish. About these beasts centred raid and counter-raid, the ambitions of kings and queens, great battles, scandalous loves, the tremendous exploits of the sagas. In a sentence, Ireland's wealth was for centuries its soft rains, its vast pasturages, those wandering herds. About this simple commerce there developed a life-mode that was at once dangerous and secure, unconcerned and anxious, reckless and rapacious, unambitious and adventurous, as peaceful and as bloody as the desert.

One has to appreciate that there were no 'clans' in Ireland. The core of the acknowledged order was the family, but the lock-knit family system did not develop. The limits of the sacred nexus were symbolized by the hand. The palm was the common ancestor; the joints of the fingers were his descendants unto his grandchildren; the fingernails were his great-grandchildren. The family was not supposed to exist beyond that.

Primogeniture was never an Irish law. The chieftainship of these family groups was a hereditary gift qualified by public election. Society was finely graded. There was not much that was democratic about it. Tradition and practice held firmly to that structure ranging slowly downward from king to slave. But it contained one satisfactory element. That 'true family-group' which has been described, known as the *deirbh-fine* (pronounced derv-finneh) lived together – early marriages made this possible. They shared property in common, grandfather and grandchildren alike, and their hold on their land was absolute and incontestable. No chief, or king, had any claim on any land other than his own. He could not legally dispossess any family in his small kingdom, which gave the families a considerable liberty of action, at any rate in theory. He could, of course, conquer and dispossess as many families outside his kingdom as he was able to snatch from a neighbouring king; he could raid and take the lands on his border; he might take neighbouring chieftains as his lieges, so that the more warlike, ambitious and able any chief of families was the nearer he approached the rank and fame of those kings whom history has preserved by name, until, if he were a really powerful man, he might alter the shape of history itself, like that Brian Boru who became king of all Ireland and defeated Danish ambitions, or that Dermot MacMurrough who, to serve his private ambitions, brought in the Normans.

From literature and history we form some idea of the lives of those 'upper classes'. The sagas glorify their lives and persons, cluster them with a jewelled magnificence through which it is difficult to visualize common reality. Thus in the tale called *The Wooing of Emer* we read a description of King Conchobar's house, the Red Branch, which goes as follows:

Nine compartments were in it from the fire to the wall. Thirty feet was the height of each *bronze partition* of the house. *Carvings* or red yew therein. A wooden floor beneath and *roofings of tiles* above. The compartment of Conchobar was in the front of the house, with a *ceiling of silver*, with *pillars of bronze*. Their *head-pieces glittered with gold* and were *set with carbuncles* so that day and night were equally light therein. There was a *gong of silver* above the king, hung from the roof-tree of the royal house. Whenever Conchobar struck the gong with his royal rod all the men of Ulster were silent. The twelve cubicles of the twelve chariot chiefs were around about the king's compartment. All the valiant warriors of the men of Ulster found space in that king's house at the time of drinking and yet no man of them could crowd the other. In it were held great and numerous gatherings of every kind and wonderful pastimes. Games and music and singing there, heroes performing their feats, poets singing, harpers and players on the timpan striking up their sounds.

Such descriptions, if they may be so called, are idealized and conventional. Not that beautiful ornaments do not remain to show us that there is a substratum of truth in these colourful pictures. But when I ask the scholars what examples we actually possess of those items that I have put into italics I am told that we have none. For the reality one has to picture a less decorative existence: the largest structures were single-room barn-like buildings with bunks or couches, in the middle a fire and its utensils, the smoke vacillating to a vent in the roof, the main ventilation through the doorways which would be closed in wild weather by pads of woven wattle, and all protected outside by one or more earthen moats – those circular raths of which many are to be seen today, all covered now with briars and brambles, preserved largely by the superstition of later ages which called them fairy-raths and feared to disturb them.

Time altered the life-mode of Ireland so very slowly that descriptions by sixteenth-century travellers are probably fairly valid for the first century. They all agree on the simplicity of Irish life as it appeared to them, much of it spent in the open air. When the Sir John Harington who translated *Orlando Furioso* visited the great Hugh O'Neill in Ulster in 1599, a cultured and travelled Irish prince who had been reared in the household of Sir Philip Sidney's father, he was entertained by O'Neill to a meal and conversation beside fern tables, on fern forms, spread under the canopy of heaven. O'Neill's children were in velvet and gold lace; his bodyguard of beardless boys were stripped to the waist. But other travellers make us see the smoke in the houses wandering indecisively to the vent; the milk strained through straw; the great candle that gutters and smells. The most part of the people dress in the famous Irish mantle, furhooded, triangular, with little underneath but a kilted shirt. Others have their long-sleeved saffron shirts of linen, breeches, shoes of skins.

Some of these observers find it all 'heathenish and savage', and some record it with a sober and respectful interest, knowing that it is an ancient and complex society, powerful, wealthy, honourable, creative in its own manner, dangerous to underestimate. Had these sixteenth-century travellers been transported back to pre-Christian times their comments would probably have been more respectful, but their pictures would not have been greatly different. Dürer's picture of Irish soldiers would probably scarcely need to be altered to depict the age of the great pagan sagas.

At no time, however, do we form any intimate picture of the life of the lower grades, largely because both letters and society were graded upwards to a caste, and both 'bards' and 'chiefs' had the aristocratic outlook. Thus, in recording the casualties at the Battle of Mag Tured, the historian opens by saying – 'I know not the number of peasants and rabble', and goes at once to the 'lords and nobles and kings' sons and overkings'; ending with – 'we reckon only a few of the servants of the overkings'. These horsemen, kernes (later, employed soldiers) were at the bottom rung of freemen: below them came the helots – men without a vote, men without a craft, inferior craftsmen, the common labourer, strangers in a district. None of these have any place in the barbarically splendid literature of the sagas, except, perhaps, as 'rabble' or as 'buffoons'. Not until the six-teenth century does anybody much care what happens to them and then it was not the Irish chiefs but the English chiefs who speak of them, in some pity and consideration.

The system as a whole, then, is not feudal. But both in prac-tice and in time the distinction balances on a knife-edge. For, as I have earlier said, ambitious dynasts, whose random forays make up the tedious and greater part of early Irish history, swarmed. In theory chiefs and kings were elected. Since, in fact, they held power partly by an atavistic loyalty to 'the ould stock', and partly by proving their worth as fighting-men and buccaneers, they depended on their lieges, or clients, and their lieges depended on them. These lieges, or clients (the Gaelic word *aur-rig*, or *urragh* literally means vice-king) were not in theory feudal vassals. They might say, or boast that they could say: 'My chief's ambitions are no concern of mine.' But in their hearts they knew quite well that the ambitions of some neigh-bouring king were definitely a great concern of theirs. And to which concern should they, at any given moment, pay the greater attention? That was always the question that affected their loyalties. Intermarriage and patronage created a royal nexus that cemented them to their traditional leader by every human bond of blood, affection, tradition and self-interest. It worked in times of peace. Militarily (and politically) the bond was fragile. One visualizes a brittle society. A large-scale border war would crack it wide open.

Thus, though Vendryes speaks of 'a free, independent and impetuous people, drunk on war and victory' he does not fail to see also that a price had to be paid for that: the price was that this life should be not only free but fractional, not only intimate but too individualist and haughty to melt into a national unity and a national organization. In three words it was aristocratic, regional and personal, and all three to an extreme degree.

It is well to insist that this indifference to political unity is a very different matter to the Celts' powerful, linguistic, and sentimental sense of racial oneness. They seem to have had no difficulty in combining this strong sense of their racial oneness with an equally strong insistence on their regional otherness; which ultimately seems to have nourished the fatal delusion that to flourish as a people it was not necessary to formulate the political concept of the nation.

In practice, as a result, a very small island was divided into five parts, called *cuigi* (the same word still means 'province' in modern Gaelic); and these fifths were further subdivided into small, fluid regions called *tuatha*. The number of people in modern Ireland who might claim to be descended from ancient kings is therefore as large as these ancient 'kings' were numberless. There was no central organization. One reads of High Kings, and there were strong men, like the famous Brian Boru, who by sheer force dominated the whole island for brief periods, but the essential factor is that there was no legal position whatsoever known as *the* Irish king.

In fact no recognized legal system (in the sense of a modern legal system) existed at all. The so-called Brehon Laws – the written laws as we have them in the manuscripts – were not a code which grew up piecemeal over centuries of disagreement and ultimate agreement, like modern case-law, nor a system developed by a national legislative. They were, quite simply, a highly idealized picture, composed 'in the study', of what popular practices and habits would be like (or might be like) in terms of law if legalists were asked by some dictator to codify

habit, practice and tradition and if he could apply sanctions to
enforce them. The Brehon Laws in other words, as we know
them, emanate from legal schools, not from any central authority. Many of them seem to be unfeasible. In so far as they depict
actual practices the evidence seems to be that these practices
varied widely according to regions.

Our picture, then, admittedly sketched in the barest outline
like a simple map or cartoon, is of an intimate, local society,
very elastic, fluid, and free, admirable and even enviable so long
as neighbours did not too bloodily spoil one another, or some
more efficient organization did not challenge it from outside.
It has been called primitive and the term has been resented,
and, up to a point (in time) rightly resented, for it not merely
worked but it was under it – as we shall see – that Ireland made
her greatest contribution to the civilization of Europe and had
one of her own most creative periods in the arts. This is a
fact that historians who judge these chronic nonconformists
by the standards of Roman or Norman discipline must not
ignore.

Those imperial-minded peoples fulfilled their genius magnificently through a corporate technique of living; these Irish also
splendidly fulfilled their genius through a technique of dis-
persion and disconnexion – up to the eleventh century, during
which long stretch of time everything they produced was
superior to the products of most of their contemporaries. But
the word 'primitive' becomes less easily refutable when the
development of most other European countries, in science, the
arts, the amenities of life, all the techniques of peace and war
begins to leave less organized countries behind in the race.

The patriotic Irish view of the conquest of Ireland by colon-
izing Britain is that her civilization was finally destroyed by a
more efficient and ruthless military organization. Perhaps it
would be more correct to say that the consolidated Tudor state
was too strong an opponent for Irish regionalism. But, if we
take the longest view of history, there was more to it even than
that. The Danes and the Normans had prepared the way, and
three things that they brought were mortal – ports, roads,
towns. From these everything followed. As well might the free-
riding Arabs of the desert have smelled disaster on seeing the

first merchants settle on their coast as the Irish, seeing the first little Danish settlements twinkle at night on the edge of the sea, have wondered whether this new devilry was not something with which they would sooner or later have to come to terms. The Irish were too arrogant and too freedom-loving to come to terms with the huckster's life. When it was too late they fought, with tremendous dash and deathless courage, but, as the system dictated, it was each man for his own horizon. They were destroyed piecemeal.

To sum up, there lay in the Irish mind, and still may lie, atavistically indestructible, an ineradicable love of individual liberty. Equality, so far as I can see, they never bothered about. They clung to the family unit because there was a good deal of individual liberty inside it. Roman Law, which was to come in with the Normans, had another idea – or had by the time the Irish met it. For in early Roman law the family system was also sacred – see the inferior position of woman, for example, subject even in her widowhood to agnates in order that the family structure might be kept intact; but as the idea of the Roman State developed the intimate idea of the Family began to yield ground to the larger concept of Society and the State. This idea never appealed to the Irish. True, the Roman State stepped in with donations of individual rights – to women for example – but when individual rights are bestowed by the State the gift is double-edged. It may be an improvement to go from domestic despotism to state paternalism; but it is, undeniably, easier to fight one's own battle with one's father than to fight it with some remote 'father', and it is, so to speak, more fun. In the Italian communes the old Germanic idea and the Roman idea were conjoined for hundreds of years in just the same uneasy way. And for the same reason, namely that the Germans brought with them from their forests that greater personal independence which always belongs to small groups, it took a long time for the Langobardic system to blend with the Roman in the great medieval and Renaissance republics.

In modern Ireland a good deal of lip-service is paid to the family-unit. If there is, in this, any backward glance at the old Celtic system it is wholly sentimental. In practice we owe all the legal rights and restrictions that we enjoy and accept to the 'brutal' Normans and the 'brutal' Tudors who are supposed to be equally responsible for the 'seven hundred years of slavery' about which our patriots often glibly talk without knowing anything much about it. If the Celtic tradition has given us anything in this field what it has given is that old atavistic individualism which tends to make all Irishmen inclined to respect no laws at all; and though this may be socially deplorable it is humanly admirable, and makes life much more tolerable and charitable and easy-going and entertaining.

PART II: THE TRUNK

POLITICAL HISTORY

c. 600–1100	*Monasticism develops. Missionaries flock to the Continent.*
c. 800	*Danish invasions begin. First coastal towns and ports.*
1014	*Battle of Clontarf checks Danish power.*
1169–	*The Normans. Many inland towns and roads. Urbanization begins.*
1200–1500	*Norman assimilation. Urbanization develops and affects the Irish life-mode. Modern sophistication begins. This period is politically blank.*
c. 1521–	*Tudor pressure begins. Reformation doctrines introduced and resisted.*

5

A BASIC CONFLICT?

WHEN the traveller today comes on tiny, ruined Romanesque churches in such lonely places as Glendalough in the Wicklow mountains, or Clonmacnoise on the Shannon, or on desolate islands about the coast, he may know that here lived either an ascetic or a student, and that here he is touching on ground that was for a long period a battleground of the Irish mind in conflict with itself.

Latin Christianity gave the Irish their first international challenge and opportunity: they took both eagerly. The first possible contemporary reference to an Irish student in exile who was also a Christian is characteristically dramatic. It is a furious reference in the letters of St Jerome (415–16) to 'an ignorant caluminator ... full of Irish porridge' who has had the insolence to criticize him.* This man was the heresiarch Pelagius, founder of Pelagianism, a man of great intellectual power. He defended himself in Jerusalem against Orosius, who had to employ an interpreter. He was in Rome before Alaric sacked it – we are now moving forward to the decay of the Roman world and stand at the brink of the Dark Ages. There Pelagius wrote his Commentaries on the Epistles of St Paul. He went on to Africa, and so on to Asia. In Jerusalem he vanishes from history. He is the great antagonist of the stern teachings of St Augustine on free-will and grace. He proclaimed the freedom of the personality and man's power to make his own soul unaided. His doctrine has persisted, in one form or another, down to the days of Jansenism and Pascal. It was partly to counter his teachings that the first St Patrick – there were, as we now know, two Patricks – caused Germanus of Auxerre to be sent to Britain and himself, later, to Ireland. The heretical views of Pelagius were highly untypical; otherwise, if he really was an Irishman,

* Some scholars maintain that Pelagius was a Briton; others that Jerome was referring to a disciple of his.

he is but one of hundreds, if not of thousands, who from the fifth to the ninth century carried into Europe not only the teachings of Christianity but a formal learning greater than Europe then possessed.

At the other end of this great period of efflorescence was that even more striking example, perhaps the greatest individual figure that the Irish presented to medieval Europe – John Eriugena (Irish-born John). He spoke Greek and Latin. He was a philosopher of considerable charm, a daring and original thinker, of whom it has been said that

while his contemporaries were only lisping in philosophy, and even his successors for centuries did no more than discuss a small number of disconnected questions, Eriugena in the ninth century worked out a complete philosophical synthesis. Apart from those incredibly daring speculations which made him the *enfant terrible* of his time he reads like a pantheistic contemporary of Saint Thomas.*

His knowledge of neo-Platonist philosophy was so intimate, indeed unique in northern Europe, that he was the only man whom Charles the Bald could find to translate a Christian neo-Platonist manuscript sent to him from Constantinople as a present from the Emperor. For Thurneysen's pregnant comment on Johannes's deep personal debt to Europe see page 54 ff.

These two men tempt us to develop the extraordinary picture of a remote island, hitherto counted as barbarian, suddenly flowering into an urbane civilization, taking back to Europe riches that might otherwise have remained buried for centuries under the ruins of the Empire. The great paleographer Traube puts the general statement in its most extreme form: 'Whoever on the continent in the days of Charles the Bald knew Greek was an Irishman, or at least his knowledge was transmitted to him through an Irishman, or the report which endows him with this glory is false.'

However, a third man reveals a very different spirit, a strain of what we might nowadays call the 'Puritanism' of the Irish mind – a strain which nothing in the romances or the lyrics foreshadow. This man is Columbanus, the great apostle of Irish

*I am guided throughout this section mainly by Kenney's *Sources for the Early History of Ireland*, Vol. I, New York, 1929. The quotation is from De Wulf, *History of Mediaeval Philosophy*, 1909, p. 167.

asceticism, to become well known abroad for his stern Monastic Rule. This counsellor of cruel self-mortification and penance – an ideal which was to run wild among the Irish cenobites – founded at Luxeuil a religious colony which was one of the germinal centres of European monasticism. And yet, although this asceticism is a disturbing and puzzling contrast with the humanism of Pelagius and the charm of Eriugena and the sweetness of many delicate notes cast elsewhere (though not typically) through the literature of the Irish Church, its founder also loved the old classical learning well enough to read – at any rate read in – Virgil and Horace, Ovid and Juvenal, may have read some of Persius and Lucan; and wrote Latin verse which has been considered remarkable for language, style and versatility.

One might, making large allowances for a personal strictness, be tempted to see here another synthesis – an intelligent Christian synthesis – if he were not also the leader of a wholesale flight to an extreme: if one did not know that around this cenobitic life which he established there grew up another vast literature whose extravagances suggest that this is but another wild oscillation in a racial mind still insufficiently experienced or trained to be able to cope with the new, Christian wonder.

The mind of the Irish people [says Kenney] during the early Christian era was, fundamentally, the product of countless ages of paganism. The popular legends (of saints and hermits), moulded under a pagan or semi-pagan attitude of mind, contained a large amalgam of magic and superstition, those survivals of primitive religion. So far, therefore, as the *acta sanctorum* depend on popular legend they are, in some degree, records of primitive religious ideas and practices. Irish paganism seems to have consisted of a lower *stratum*, deep and wide, of magical belief and practice, and, superimposed thereon, an upper section of mythology. Myth and magic were ejected from their positions of supremacy by the coming of Christianity, but the evidence does not indicate that the sphere of operation of either was extensively diminished.*

And he points to the curious fact that it is in the later medieval texts that this pagan survival is most marked; as if Christianity,

---

*Op. cit., p. 302. On the saint as the new 'medicine-man'.

in becoming more and more widely accepted, became debased accordingly.

Christianity thus restates the internal imaginative and political struggle in an intellectual form. Where that little ruined church is alone and remote, or where there are merely rude stone cells as on the precipitous Skellig Rock, miles out in the Atlantic, one may presume saintly hermits, asceticism, magic fables; where a round tower's grey finger points to the sky one may safely presume a larger settlement, a larger church and streets of bothies, and one is likely to come on traditions of a famous cenobitic school of learning. Can the two notes be harmonized? Or are they completely antithetical?

Here one must pause to note another immense problem rooted in that characteristic regionalism at which we have glanced in the chapter called 'The Social Reality'. When monasticism became the regular Irish church system the effect was against episcopal or diocesan organization and for rule by local abbots, chosen (as in the secular society of the *deirbh-fine* or true family) from blood-relations of the local founder, with the inevitable regionalist autonomy reaffirmed by bonds of blood between the regional ruler and the regional monastery and its regional offshoots. That abuses would arise out of this lack of centralization was natural. For example, to give but one, the heirship (called the *co-arb*ship) of St Patrick at Armagh had, by the twelfth century, passed by hereditary succession for fifteen generations, and in eight cases had been filled by married laymen.

Perhaps the deeper truth here, however, is not so much concerned with Irish monasticism as with monasticism as a system anywhere, though the dangers were aggravated in Ireland by peculiar local conditions. The virtues inherent in monastic systems admittedly do require autonomy in order to flourish. The monk is, however, merely the leaven not the loaf. The orders have accordingly had their heyday and their dogday. In their heyday they might be given full rein. It was necessary in their decline to merge them back quickly into the general discipline of Christendom. Meanwhile it was above all necessary that a strong parent church should keep a careful watch lest these outliers should be exploited by the secular forces about them. In early medieval Ireland there was no such organized parent church to do this. The old regionalist, local, personal Irish passion for blood and place ran riot until the Normans completed the reformation of church government.

Why did the Irish seize so wholeheartedly on the Columban form of monasticism? To quote Kenney again –

The decisive reason for the dominance of monasticism in Ireland was, we may be sure, the *enthusiasm* with which the early Irish Christians embraced the cenobitical life and the ideals of asceticism; this it was that provided inmates, sometimes in their thousands, for all the monasteries and, as the spirit of asceticism grew, sent Irish anchorites to seek hermitages on the islands of the Irish and Scottish coasts or overseas in foreign lands.*

From the sixth to the twelfth century the exploits of these new heroes were heroic to the point of extravagance, a medley of more or less pointless peregrinations and penances, often repulsive, at any rate to modern minds; of prolonged pilgrimages; of true evangelization; and of valuable secular teaching. Many Irishmen wandered to the East, to Iceland, to their own most stormtorn islands, for no reason but Abraham's urge to self-banishment in God's name. *Egredere de terra tua et de cognatione tua.* Kenney, illustrating how this sacrifice of their dearest associations seems to have appealed in a peculiar manner to the Irish, aptly quotes this entry in the *Anglo-Saxon Chronicle*:

Three Irishmen came to King Alfred in a boat without any oars, from Ireland, whence they had stolen away because they desired, for the love of God, to be in a state of pilgrimage – *they reckoned not where.*

One must not be tempted by the bizarre tales of the extreme *penitentes* into giving them too much of the picture. Yet, although the legends about them are quite unreliable as to detail their popularity must suggest that they offered at least one ideal. Thus one of them is supposed to have condemned himself never to scratch; another is said to have hung from hooks under his armpits for seven years (the usual magical number); of another it is said that 'he used to lie the first night in the same grave with every corpse brought to his church'; another is said to have sat for the usual seven years on the backbone of a whale.

* Kenney, op. cit., p. 293.

And so on. The alleged practice known as *virgines subintroductae* may not be authentic – the habit of bringing beautiful girls into the cell of a saintly aspirant in order to give him the glory of overcoming the agonies of lust. St Ita was said to have kept a stagbeetle 'as big as a lapdog a-sucking her until it ate away one of her sides'.

One does not wish to propose a bald antinomy between asceticism and learning. They were often mingled in the same man – I have mentioned the clear example of Columbanus. But one cannot deny that some sort of struggle was going on through all those centuries between a sane discipline (under Christian and Classical influence) and a hardly sane one (under the old extravagant, pagan influence). One might even call it a struggle between the new foreign classicism and the old native romanticism. Or one might push things farther still and see here a struggle between Reason and Imagination. However we phrase it what is at stake all the time is a definition of order. That the antitheses never mingled lastingly is not surprising. Asceticism restricts, Classicism perfects. Both attempt to order. But the one order is barren and the other is creative. Above all the one is local and particular and the other is panoramic and general – and there was hardly any urge in this medieval Irish thought towards the general. (Even the jurists show no art of generalization; for whenever asked a general question, such as 'What is Justice?' they will reply by enumerating 'There are fifteen of Justice.'

An incapacity to generalize? Can one seize on it as a clue to the nature of those conflicts in the early Irish mind that we so easily sense but find it so difficult to define? There is a remarkable observation by one of the greatest of Celtic scholars, Rudolph Thurneysen, which forcibly tempts one to seize on it. Struck, as so many others have been, by the strange fact that, from beginning to end, the native Irish tradition produced only one (certain) Irish philosopher – that Johannes Eriugena whom I have already mentioned – and observing that certain Irish grammatical tracts with which he was concerned could never define in general terms but, instead, always fell back on particular examples, he made this comment on those many grammarians and on that solitary philosopher:

The Irishman regards the concepts of grammar as concrete facts. There are, indeed, few documents which give us such a deep insight into the mentality of the ancient Irish. . . . It is only by comparison with them that we can measure the vastness of the world of ideas which a man like Johannes Eriugena was able to master. . . . Such a work as his *De Divisione Natura* would have been impossible in the Ireland of his day and would not even have had a chance of being understood. It is true that the Irish added to their piety a zeal for learning rarely found on the continent . . . but only in closer proximity to the Mediterranean were they able to develop as rational thinkers.*

Is this our password to the nature, conflicts and limitations of the Irish mentality during its most formative centuries? Too concrete? The idea is temptingly neat. Yet I feel that it is too neat and it certainly is not universally true. It does not, for example, at all fit in with the plastic arts of early and medieval Ireland. To see this we need do no more than turn page after page of Françoise Henri's three splendid volumes, *L'art Irlandais*. In those volumes the pictures show early and medieval Irish art not as a 'concrete' art but as a patently abstract art. Indeed, if I read her correctly, one of the sources of Mlle Henri's love and admiration for these works of art, which we all share, is her feeling that Irish artists avoided the concrete (or representational) not because they could not compass it, but because they did not want to be limited by it.

Take a single instance – the splendid high cross of Moone. There is, on one side of the base, a figuration of the loaves from St Mark's narrative of the miracle of the loaves and the fishes. To suggest the loaves the sculptor has carved a number of solid circles in high relief. Their pattern is delightful and effective. But as for being in any sense 'concrete' – that is, concerned with actual loaves rather than abstractions of loaves – they might just as well be platters, cymbals, drums, bowls or wheels. Nobody would wish that even one speck of that superb high cross had been fashioned otherwise. He will, however, recognize that this was the way in which the Irish sculptors wanted to work from the very beginning. There are, indeed, a few delightful semi-actualist carvings of heads in stone and metal – the best on

the Irish Romanesque doorway of Dysert O'Dea, or the figur-
ines on the Brac Maodhog in the National Museum. Yet even
these beautiful carvings are highly stylized, Byzantine, decorative and symbolical rather than concrete and representational.
To look at them in any other way is to apply to them criteria
which do not belong to their own preferred mode.

In short the early Irish mind was neither concrete nor imaginative – it was both: concrete when thinking and imaginative when creating; the one a limitation, the other a release; each contradicting rather than complementing the other;
perhaps, in the long run, each enfeebling the other – for even
artists have to think, experiment, rebel, explore new ways of
doing old things, get down to principles, theorize, argue endlessly, or else become bogged down in some convention that,
however beautiful and effective, must ultimately exhaust itself,
which was what happened to medieval Irish art. Had later
generations of Irish artists chosen or been able to break from
their original conventions, had Irish art as a whole developed
later in some other way, these early conventions would not be
so racially revealing. We would merely say, 'This was how
they *began* to achieve'. As we do of the arts in Europe, which
also in their beginnings, produced equally beautiful and moving
things in a not dissimilar convention, and then in the twelfth,
but above all in the thirteenth century, broke through the cul de
sac of Byzantine symbolism and near-abstraction into the full-
blooded realism of the carvings of the cathedrals of Strasbourg,
Rouen or Orvieto – after which the road was wide open for the
development of European art as we now know it.

One is naturally tempted to say that such a purely Irish development was prevented by the Viking raids and the Norman
invasions, and they must have, to some extent, interfered with
it. But the raids ceased in 1014 with the total defeat of the Vik-
ings at the Battle of Clontarf; and the Normans did not effectively control at any time more than one-sixth of the island and
were soon assimilated. From the time of their settling down to
the coming of the Tudors, 'with brimstone, fire and sword',
the Irish artist, if not the Irish swordsman, had a century and
a half of at least comparative peace and freedom to develop in
any way he wished. His real enemy, however, was not turbu-

lence. It was his remoteness from all these seminal influences that were meanwhile fructifying the arts of the Continent. Who can say what might have happened to his work had he been less remote? Or how Irish thinking might have developed had it always been 'in closer proximity to the Mediterranean'? But one shies off such imponderable hypotheses, left, perforce, only with our awareness that there was from the start some antithetical block, conflict or disorder in the Irish nature that prevented both artists and scholars from developing their potential to the full.

There is nothing imponderable about the disorder of their background. As a religious system the failure of Irish monasticism was in the end so complete that the first real Norman 'invasion' of Ireland was a movement of necessary church reform directed from Canterbury. By then (eleventh century) the Cluniac reform had already applied elsewhere its well-known ideals of organization, uniformity and discipline. Archbishop Lanfranc now directed it towards Ireland. The reformers were familiar enough with continental irregularities but they were particularly shocked by conditions here. The main evil, as I have already intimated, was, as indeed it had been elsewhere, the secular intrusion. In too many foundations the abbot had by the eleventh century become a lay lord, the monks his tenants, the students mere labourers and the priests hired servants. The Norman observers speak, too, of lax morality* – monks and priests marrying, the laity living loose lives, but this is debatable and the animadversions of Lanfranc and St Bernard may have arisen, at least in part, from unfamiliarity with traditional Irish marriage customs.† Church discipline was undoubtedly lax. There were, it is true, many bishops in Ireland, but it is the final measure of their helplessness that there was, for them, no controlling, ordering power.

Lanfranc asserted his supremacy over the Irish and encouraged native reformers to establish an episcopal system. The Hiberno-Danish sees in the coastal towns of Dublin, Wexford, Waterford and Limerick eagerly agreed and sent their priests

*See Kenney, op. cit. pp. 745ff.
† See Orpen, *Ireland under the Normans*, Vol. 1, p. 124, on the position of women.

to Canterbury to be consecrated. Others, equally anxious to re-
gularize their position in the universal church, set up chapters,
cathedral centres, provinces, and new monasteries under foreign
monks. The corporate system thus enters, for the time effectively, on the regional Irish scene through religion and invasion.

6

THE NORMAN GIFT

IN the patriotic iconography of nineteenth-century Ireland the constant motifs were the round tower, the Celtic cross, the wolf-hound, the harp, and the ruined abbey. But for some reason, connected no doubt with the idea that the 'enslavement' of Ireland began when Dermot MacMurrough, King of Leinster, brought in the foreigner, that is, the Normans, another one of the commonest features of the Irish landscape is generally omitted – the ruined Norman castle or keep.

One sees these wrecks of time from the train and from the road all over the country, but most commonly in the east and south, ivy-covered, perhaps no more than a broken tooth of masonry, a shelter for cattle on wet days, or a monument carefully preserved by the Board of Works. If this book were a political history we would have to deal under this head with the 'seven-hundred-years of slavery', beginning with those Norman conquerors' castles. Since this is a journey in the track of a mind our interest is the immense gifts the Normans have brought to that amalgam of many strains which is modern Ireland. To us the Norman castle is a relic of a civilization.

The Norman invasion was, to begin, the private gamble of a small group of adventurers. Later on the gamble became, under Henry II and his successors, an effort at national colonization or conquest – which was, however, never completed. The first cluster of adventurers that landed at Bannow Bay, in Wexford, on 1 May 1169, consisted of thirty knights, sixty other horsemen, and about three hundred archers on foot. Within nine months they and their Irish allies had taken the walled town of Wexford from the Ostmen, subdued Dublin, and made themselves virtual masters of all Leinster. The overt reason for their success was twofold: the lack of an effective Irish centre to organize opposition – or, though we Irish do not much care for the bitter word, Irish disunity; the second reason was superior Norman military technique.

The Irish simply could not realize what was happening. When, later, one king after another made his obeisances to Henry they thought that it 'meant no more than the similar acknowledgement which they had often given, and broken, to an *ard-ri* (or High King). Nay, as Henry would be far off across the seas, they probably expected it to mean a great deal less'.* It soon became a case of Less is More. They had been for so long accustomed to giving hostages, often their own sons, if needs be sacrificing them to death or to blinding when agreements had to be broken, that they thought that the same feckless technique would work with these strangers. It proved to be a very different matter when these practised mail-clad knights set up stone castles, created towns, held what towns there were (whenever the Irish, who had a claustrophobic horror of towns, took one, right up to the seventeenth century, they burned or abandoned it), and from these centres enforced their bonds.

This widespread sprouting of towns was the most fruitful thing the Normans did. They began civic life in Ireland. With roads and ports trade followed. They established abbeys in numbers. The result was a new urbanity, a new and more elaborate life-mode, new skills and a new sweetness, for which the old Celtic world paid in blood, havoc and unrest. The little chieftains were slaughtered and robbed; the more important chieftains submitted to terms, accepted portions of their former territories and continued to rule there according to Irish law. At least one is known to have become a feudal lord, indistinguishable from his Norman neighbours; and there may have been more like him. Many interspersed Irish districts remained, living the old life-mode, fearful, restless and vengeful. The actual labourers remained where they were. They were on the whole no worse off materially, and probably some of them were happier as villeins than they had been as Irish serfs.

One can still feel this Norman influence. It hangs almost palpably in the air of some parts of the country, distinctive and unmistakable, chiefly in the east and south-east. In such counties as Kilkenny, where this influence lasted long and was least disturbed, even by the disastrous upheaval of the

*Orpen, op. cit., I, 284.

Reformation,* the very nature of the people is patently different to that of the contiguous county of Tipperary. Even the people of south Tipperary, which was more effectively colonized than north Tipperary, appear, to me at any rate, clearly affected by that prolonged foreign reign.

Where the invaders established abbeys this influence was and is most pronounced. I happen to have made a study of one such district, that around the present village of Graiguena-managh on the River Barrow, in County Kilkenny, the site of a Cistercian Abbey called *De Valle Sancti Salvatoris*, founded by William the Marshal in the twelfth century. Within living memory one could have found almost every necessary craft being still practised in this tiny village – boat-building, nail-making, weaving, boot-making, bacon-curing, the making of salt, starch and candles, tanning, a small foundry, wheelwrights, carpenters, joiners, tinsmiths, bakers, coopers, quilters, and so on. In the rich country around, the farmhouses have an air rather of Wessex than of Ireland, solid cutstone barns, finely arched, with all the marks of a tradition of good husbandry, such as old trees, straight ditches, orchards and kitchen gardens. There is all over the land the fragrance of a long memory of stable conditions, so different to the harsh south and west where the generations have lived for centuries from hand to mouth and have only in our own time cut free from the gnaw-ing fear of poverty and famine. For the story of many parts of Ireland there are no records: here there are many; rent-rolls and charters that take us back to the Middle Ages. Nor was this region on the River Barrow fortunate simply because the soil was rich. When the first Cistercians from Wiltshire stood on the hills above the river and saw what they had to cope with they called it 'a place of horror and vast solitude', dark with wood and scrub and the threat of lawless men. They had to work the valley to make it profitable.

Or the traveller should visit the modern city of Kilkenny with its beautiful twelfth-thirteenth-century cathedral, and its other Norman remains. Although its ancient round tower and frag-ments of a Romanesque church show that it had a pre-Norman

---

* It may be well to remember that the Norman invasion, unlike the Tudor invasion, was carried out by Catholics.

life as a religious centre its expansion and civil importance dates from 1192 when the first castle of the Marshals was built. It has flourished ever since and is, so far as I know, the only such town or city that has, like so many English cathedral towns, grown under the wings of abbey and of manor, adapting itself graciously to Time without wholly losing its original quality.

To make another of my forward leaps, the contrast with the ultimate fate of that village and abbey of Graiguenamanagh is pointed. This village, far from continuing to cluster for shelter under the protecting wings of the old abbey – said by one traveller to have been, even in its ruin, as beautiful as Tintern – has, in the most amazing, terrifying and thorough fashion, crept over the abbey, stock and stone, built garage and pub, warehouse and shop, stye and police barracks on top of, in and with its fallen stones, so that, today, this ancient memorial of Norman civilization lies like a drowned glory beneath a little Irish village, and no casual traveller would notice anything, until, by halting for a few days, he would gradually become aware of an aura not of our time. Searching, then, he will come upon the poor stones from which it emanates.

The point of the contrast is, ultimately, political. It marks the beginning of the central Irish tragedy. The Normans did not give to the Irish the benefits of their own laws. So little did they realize, as the Danish kings realized when they conquered Britain, that the keystone of a successful colonization is a blending of races, which is in turn dependent on the rule of equal rights for all before the law, that it was no felony in Norman-Irish law to kill an Irishman. The fact that it was, in effect, no felony for an Irishman to kill a Norman has nothing to do with the principle of the matter, though Orpen is, no doubt, right in seeing at the root of this fatal error of statesmanship the fact that the Normans, in their ignorance of Ireland, regarded the Irish as uncouth and barbarous, as the Tudors were to do after them. Since the military conquest was far from complete, for it was firm only in the east, weak in the south, and scarcely touched the north and west, one may imagine the result. Add to this discrimination the greatest weakness of all, that the foreign ruler lived in another country, was always otherwise engaged, 'and, indeed, in the person of King John, was not morally equipped, either to rule his (Irish) barons with justice or to restrain them from harsh treatment of his Irish subjects'.

By the time of the Reformation a typical village and abbey like this Graiguenamanagh was no longer pure Norman. If Lynch's famous epigram that the Normans became *Hiberniores Hibernicis ipsis* (more Irish than the Irish themselves), is an overstatement, it contains an historical truth — that Ireland, whether Norman or Gaelic, went as much of its own way as 'the alternate neglect and capricious interference' of the *Dominus Hiberniae* would allow it to go; and, as we know, at the Reformation Ireland went, as it had always gone, along the road of the old faith. Abbeys and cathedral-churches in Britain might then, with exceptions, continue under the new dispensation. In Ireland the exception was the other way round. The abbey, abandoned and neglected, ultimately tumbled in on itself. As the village throve the abbey vanished. Its influence remains, masked and muffled, symbol of the incompleteness of the Norman conquest itself. But one need not go to any such town or village for these symbols. Many a ruined Norman castle, with its sheltering cows, is all that remains of an influence whose memory is otherwise only preserved by local tradition, parchments in a museum, humps of grass.

The simplest illustration of the masked influence is, of course, in our surnames. Burkes are Norman De Burgos, and Fitzgerald, Power, Joyce, Coady, Tracy, Costello, Butler, Barry, and others more Gaelic-seeming, like MacAveely, are likewise Norman. The late Edmund Curtis, Professor of History in Dublin University, an authority on the period, in a cursory study estimated that at least a seventh of the commonest Irish surnames are Norman. Wherever, he said, one meets the round compact head, the pale complexion, sturdy build, square face, fine nose, falcon- rather than eagle-like, such as we saw in the Irish leader John Redmond, one meets the true Norman type. The mental characteristics are emotional control, conservation of energies, restrained idealism, a certain closeness, frugal yet open-handed, 'traders rather than industrialists, safe rather than speculative', imagination well in hand, a good deal of self-reliance, people sometimes vindictive and always stubborn. Curtis thought them *rusé* and full of wile. The strain is now so much mingled and watered that one no more meets a pure Norman than one can find a pure Celt. Still, this is not the list of qualities that one would think of when speaking of the more Gaelic parts of Ireland where character is so much more ebullient and unpredictable, and passion less controlled.

It was the Normans who first introduced the Irish mind to politics. They were our first Home Rulers. They did not think of Ireland as a nation, least of all as their nation, or bother about such symbols as Language, and they had no interest in ancient traditions, but they did stand as sturdily for their religion and 'their' land as, in the nineteenth century, an O'Connell for the one and a Davitt for the other; by which time, of course, Norman and Irish were completely commingled. They initiated politics as the word was to be understood in Ireland to the end of the Irish Parliamentary Party in 1922.

The first foreign-imposed Irish Parliament met in 1297. In passing acts forbidding Normans to dress or wear their hair long, like the Irish, or to maintain Irish foot-soldiers or *kernes*, and in applying the term 'degenerate English' to such as did, it shows the way the wind was already blowing. They were being merged; it was also felt in London that they were simultaneously becoming too powerful. Both tendencies are illustrated by the two De Burgos of Connacht who frankly rejected feudal law in favour of the old Gaelic law of male succession in order to get possession of their father's lands in Galway and Mayo. They thereby founded the two great lines of the Clanrickard Burkes and the Mayo Burkes who, without any legal title, were lords of the west up to the middle of the sixteenth century – when the Tudor conquerors were to curse and scorn 'the beggarly Burkes' as heartily and bitterly as they ever cursed any Gael. The same thinning of what Curtis aptly calls 'the feudal veneer' might be illustrated by many other examples. It was to check this movement that official after official was sent to Ireland, and in resistance to these that the descendants of the first colonists persistently raised the claims of their own native caste to rule Ireland from within. The distance in time is great to Grattan's 'Patriot Parliament', to the fight of the Anglo-Irish upper classes against the legislative Union of Ireland and Great Britain in the eighteenth century, but the sentiment and the technique of those movements have here their common origin.

The native Irish paid no overt attention whatever to these political démarches of the Norman colonists, but they could not go on for ever ignoring the *fact*, and the fact was to become their deepest inner tension, their abiding obsession – to be summed up as 'the English enemy'. There was not a month when this animus was not blown upon in some part or other of the island and the eyes of the more thoughtful turned towards the east. For, even if the Irish took no specific interest in Anglo-Irish politics, they were obliged to adapt themselves to its effects. If the Normans tended to become Irishized, the Irish were gradually forced to become more and more feudal. One sees this in the adoption of the feudal right of the son to succeed the father, which virtually changed the Gaelic chiefs, or the 'captains of nations', or 'lords of countries', as the English legal phrases called them, into Gaelic barons. One sees the feudalization of their minds, too, in their introduction of standing armies and mercenaries, chiefly nationalized Norse from the Scottish isles. Apart from the old rule of the chieftains' limited ownership of land their power was thus to become more and more arbitrary. In one way and another the generations (for the process was of the slowest) were obliged, too, to deal with what the eighteenth century called Dublin, the nineteenth called 'Dublin Castle', and our time calls 'the Government', that central power which in all centuries from then to now it was their concern to pacify or to circumvent. In those centuries their technique was one of resistance to the limit, always too local to be effective or lasting, followed by feigned submissions and simulated friendship.

One pauses to consider that one of the fondest Irish delusions is that we are a guileful people. We expect guile from one another as we expect rain from our skies. When, however, we do meet guile or rain in other lands we are a little pained. We are especially taken aback if we find that England is either wetter or more wily than Ireland. It is possible that other countries share our delusion. It may be not shock but disappointment which has produced the epithet 'perfidious Albion'. It may seem on the surface that in those frequent submissions exacted by English kings, and more or less readily made by the Irish kings with little intention of implementing them, the English were wasting and the Irish purchasing valuable time. Twice, for example, Richard II came in person to Ireland to receive the homage of the paramount chiefs, in return for which they were in 1395 at last admitted as legal possessors of the land they had always ruled – a considerable triumph for them at the period – and against which they, on their side, agreed to surrender lands they had been 'usurping' from the barons. Practically, nothing at all would seem to have happened except that Richard went on his way rejoicing.

But empires can afford to take their time, and an invaded people cannot, and things did happen beneath the surface. Curtis rightly points out that it is significant that after that imposing and solemn submission of 1395 the greater Irish chiefs dropped the title of 'king', so that henceforth, for example, MacCarthy is not 'King of Desmond' but 'The MacCarthy More'. The Irish had not surrendered only land; they had surrendered some portion of their minds, their memories, their traditional outlook. As this is a non-political history it is not our business to consider whether it might not have been far better if they had either united and fought, or honestly submitted and settled down with the Norman barons to create a Norman-Irish island to balance against that Anglo-Norman island across the sea. Since they neither did one thing nor the other, one can only observe that the upshot of it was that they introduced themselves to politics under the worst possible definition and under the worst possible conditions – that is to say, without any intellectual idea or any moral purpose – in a word, opportunistically.

The Normans brought other less Grecian gifts to the Irish mind. They brought into the landlocked lagoon of Gaelic literature welcome gushes from the world's seas. From this period come most of the Gaelic translations of European literature that we possess, mainly classical and Arthurian tales and poems – Irish versions of *The Romance of the Grail*, *Marco Polo*, Virgil's *Aeneid*, the *Trojan Wars*, the *Odyssey*, the medieval English romances of Guy of Warwick and Bevis of Hampton, the *Travels of Maundeville*, the legend of the Minotaur. But the most charming of all gifts was the elaborate

convention of Provençal love-poetry which the Gaelic poets skil-
fully adapted to their own formal traditions, indeed absorbed
into them. Here, as in the early lyrics, is again a perfect synthesis – confined, alas, to this one small field – a synthesis this
time between Europe and Ireland, between the graceful formalities of a new society and the wild passions of an old one,
greatly exciting in its suggestion of what might have come
from a complete wedding of Norman and Gael.

One poem, in fine translation from the Gaelic by Padraic
Colum, will give us an example of this new departure:

> O woman, shapely as the swan,
> On your account I shall not die.
> The men you've slain – a trivial clan –
> Were less than I.
>
> I ask me shall I die for these;
> For blossom-teeth and scarlet lips?
> And shall that delicate swan-shape
> Bring me eclipse?
>
> Well-shaped the breasts and smooth the skin
> The cheeks are fair, the tresses free;
> And yet I shall not suffer death,
> God over me.
>
> Those even brows, that hair like gold,
> Those languorous tones, that virgin way;
> The flowing limbs, the rounded heel
> Slight men betray.
>
> Thy spirit keen through radiant mien,
> Thy shining throat and smiling eye,
> Thy little palm, thy side like foam –
> I cannot die.
>
> O woman, shapely as the swan,
> In a cunning house hard-reared was I;
> O bosom white, O well-shaped palm
> I shall not die.

That is but one note or convention out of many. And yet, perhaps, it may be more than a convention, more than one move

in the game of *amour courtois*, like the movement of refusal in certain amorous dances that end in fore-ordained surrender and passion. It may be that there is something in G. K. Chesterton's comment that this is 'the hardness of the real Irishman', for whom love is no game – as it was not for Dermot MacMurrough who burnt another Ilium for O'Rourke's wife. It may not be just a blind shot for Chesterton to say that the 'curt, bleak words' (though bleak is certainly not the right adjective) 'come out of the ancient Ireland of cairns and fallen kings' and 'a haughty, heathen spirit'. Whether heathen or Christian there is at any rate a something different about many of them when set side by side with Provençal verse; as in that wild poem about the woman torn between two loves, her poet-lover and her husband, of which Dr Robin Flower wrote that

it is the last in a long series of poems, like the Old Woman of Beare and Liadain and Cuirthir, in which a figure or a situation of passion is realised with an absolute and final intensity. Such poems as these would alone justify the study of Irish literature, for their like is not to be found elsewhere, and their disappearance would be a loss not only to Ireland but to the whole world.*

There was one other bond between the Normans and the Irish. It deserves a brief chapter to itself.

*The Gaelic anthology of these poems is *Dánta Grádha*. Edited and collected by Tomás O'Rathaile, Cork, 1926. Translations in *Love's Bitter Sweet*, by Robin Flower, Cuala Press, Dublin, 1925.

7

THE RELIGIOUS STRAIN

POTENTIALLY the most fruitful bond between Norman and Irish was religion. Unfortunately it had no direct political carry-over. The Normans had Norman priests, the Irish had Irish priests. The famous Statutes of Kilkenny 1366, the most outstanding Norman effort to keep 'the two nations' apart, had, among other things, excluded Irish clerics from English houses and benefices. But religion alone could never have united the people, never have overridden their other, deeper loyalties. The Catholics of the Pale, that secure English land in the east radiating out from Dublin would, for example, never have joined the rest of the island in a Catholic enterprise against England. Religion alone would not have been enough to bind even the Irish. When, in the sixteenth century, the Desmonds of the south rose in a war of revolt which took on the nature of a Holy War, the O'Neills of the north rode on the English side against them. It is futile to consider whether what we nowadays call 'nationality' would, without religion, have united the Irish since the term as yet meant nothing to them. They had the old sentimental feeling of otherness but, as yet, no political concept of nationalism to canalize it.

What religion did effect, however, was of paramount importance in modern Irish orientations. It turned the Irish mind to Rome and Spain. That movement outward was to do much to enlarge the Irish mind, to give it something of a world outlook, although, ultimately, the association of loyalty to Rome and resistance to Britain was to merge in a manner not very satisfactory to either.

But this is merely to read one of our forward-pointing signposts at a crossroads in history. Having read the warning inscription, and glanced at the rough country ahead, let us return our eyes to the fourteenth century and look around the terrain. We have come far from the first stages of the invasion under

Henry II and see ahead the bulky shadow of Henry VIII. The
Irish Church has formally accepted the Irish monarch as
Dominus Hiberniae (from the time of Henry II: Synod of
Cashel, 1171), a synod which put the coping-stone on the long
work of reform but accompanied it with submission to the English king. It regulated marriages, baptisms, tithes; established
finally that long-needed episcopal and parochial organization;
ended native liturgies – 'The divine offices shall be celebrated
according to the use of the Church of England'; it submitted
to Henry. Within one hundred and fifty years, however, in
1317, at the time of the invasion of Ireland by Edward Bruce
of Scotland, a combination of Irish chiefs had to send a Grand
Remonstrance to the Pope at Avignon, charging the English
kings with (among secular cruelties and injustices) the wrongs
done to the Irish Church. This date may mark the clear beginning
of the split. It develops when the Papacy intervened to prevent
the operation of that Statute of Kilkenny which differentiated
between Irish priest and Norman priest, an intervention which
had the natural effect of attracting the sympathies of the greatest
number towards Rome.

The situation could not develop clearly for over two hundred
years after that because the Church in Ireland, taken as a whole,
became more and more disunited and disorganized. On the eve
of the Reformation it had fallen back into a state of 'spiritual
and intellectual stagnation'. 'Abuses of every description pre-
vailed.' '... Some of [the clergy] were openly immoral and
many of them had not sufficient learning to preach or instruct
their flocks.'*

* The first two of these quotations are from *Church and State in Tudor
Ireland*, R. Dudley Edwards, London, 1935. The third is from MacCaffrey,
History of the Catholic Church from the Renaissance to the Revolution, as
quoted by Edwards. The whole of Edwards's Introduction should be read,
but I think he is unfair to blame the Normans for so many purely Irish
evils. Thus, Edwards: 'It was the Normans who introduced armour and
stone fortresses. It was through the Normans that they [The Irish] began to
burn churches and despoil their enemies.' Alas, they despoiled themselves
let alone their (foreign) enemies hundreds of years before the Normans
came; and was it not rather weak of them if they did see a Norman burn
a church and said, 'What a good idea!' Doubtless the Normans and the
Irish learned both good and bad from each other. It is tiresome when
nations blame one another for their own faults.

It was not until the sixteenth century that religion began to be identified, however ambiguously, with patriotic resistance, partly under the pressure of the Reformation and partly under the effective evangelizing work of the mendicant orders who, when scattered by the suppression of their houses, went far and wide preaching at once loyalty to Rome and revolt against the English.

Nothing, to risk an Irish bull, could be more illuminating than this ambiguity. For the first real Catholic uprising was led, not by the Irish, but by one of the most powerful of the old Norman families – the southern Desmonds – and it arose, in the first place, out of economic pressure. Necessity had locked the Desmonds into the Irish system: they had come to depend for their great power and revenue on their Gaelic tenants who, in the characteristic fashion of the period, lived outwardly by feudal and inwardly by Gaelic loyalties and customs. When Gerald, the fourteenth earl of Desmond, was held prisoner in London for his failure to suppress this Gaelic life-mode and pay the Queen her full feudal dues, his cousin Sir James Fitzmaurice got himself elected captain of his people and went to the Continent to raise a great Catholic confederacy, backed by Philip II and the Pope, against the oppressions of the English. He returned to Ireland in 1579 with some small aid from Spain and a Bull from the Pope which declared Elizabeth deprived of both her kingdoms. That date, 1579, is the operative date for the effective beginning of a new, and thenceforward indissoluble merger of two ideas whose slogan has ever since powerfully dominated the Irish mind – Faith and Fatherland.*

The Desmond revolt was crushed bloodily. It was followed by one of the first of several big Plantations. These have to be mentioned because they meant a further cross-breeding, a further dilution of Celtic blood. What other reasons, hidden in the mists of time, there may be for the many differences in character between the peoples of various parts of Ireland one cannot tell. The Norman strain in and about Kilkenny and Carlow may not alone account for the individual quality of

* For a brilliant and moving account of Fitzmaurice's war the reader should not fail to read *The Celtic Peoples and Renaissance Europe*, by David Mathew.

those counties; the Danish background may not alone explain Wexford; the Scottish infusion Antrim; nor may it wholly explain the qualities of the Cork people that settlers such as Sir Walter Raleigh brought in a transfusion of Devon and Somerset blood. All we know is that these mixtures did occur and would have had their effects, and that as time goes on and cross-breeding flourishes, we will have to agree that too many strains and influences have been woven into the tapestry of the Irish mind for anybody to disentangle them all.

Religion has thus, at the end of a long and tangled period, made Norman and Irish comrades in distress if in nothing else. But, as we have seen, religion did not and could not do this unaided. It was welded with politics and not unaffected by economic stress. It became, in Fitzmaurice's hands, a standard for a common dissatisfaction with English rule, the first metaphor, the first symbol, of an emergent bud of political nationalism.

PART III: THE SIX BRANCHES

1556 *First Plantations or Colonizations.*

1586 *Collapse of Desmond Insurrection. Plantation of Munster. A peasant tenantry begins to emerge.*

1592 *First Irish University founded.*

1603 *Collapse of Tyrone (O'Neill) Insurrection. Plantation of Ulster. End of the old Gaelic order.*

1652 *Cromwellian Plantations.*

1691 *End of Williamite wars. More confiscations.*

1700 *The 'Bad Century' begins. Death of Gaelic literature. The Penal Laws. Rise of Anglo-Irish culture.*

1791 *The United Irishmen. Wolfe Tone. The Rebel emerges as a type.*

1801 *Legislative Union of Great Britain and Ireland.*

1829 *Daniel O'Connell wins emancipation for the Catholics. Rise of modern Irish Democracy. Political power of the Priest begins.*

1841 *The Young Irelanders. Modern Irish writing begins.*

1875 *Rise of Charles Stewart Parnell. The peasant tenantry strengthen their position.*

1916 *The last insurrection.*

1922 *Founding of the Irish Free State.*

8

THE NEW PEASANTRY

A MODERN Irish critic once suggested that the three dominant notes of the Irish consciousness are Land, Religion and Nationality. (As will be seen I count six such notes, or branches.) So far in this history of the Irish consciousness we have seen only the faint outlines of Religion and Nationalism coming to the surface of the pool, though, as yet, mere gleams that, at the time, nobody could have christened. Land, land-hunger, land-passion, land-love, and the author and creature of that love, the peasant, have as yet made no appearance. As I have said, the literature of the old Gaelic world did not — to use a modern word — feature the simple folk. It shows no interest in common folk. They had no Langland.

The first people to proclaim even an interest in them were not native Irish but invading English who were shocked at their condition — though, to be sure, a political interest urged this human interest, and what mainly displeased these colonists no doubt was that these poor flies, as they called them, were so caught in the web of oppression of their native chiefs (as indeed they by now were) as to be undetachable from their schemes. It is none the less true that the small 'tenants' were much put upon by their lords. Under the old Gaelic system they had been at least to some degree independent; under this latter-day Gaelic-Norman semi-feudal system they had hardly any moral or immoral compensations — such as a share in the spoils — for the increasing exactions of their chieftains. With those earlier compensations the 'tenant' had once been content to entertain fighting-men quartered on him, or give military service himself: when, without them, it happened too often, when it seemed to him part and parcel of his general struggling insecurity, he would have welcomed a fixed rent from any overlord, as in the nineteenth century his descendants certainly did. He was offered exactly this by the Queen's deputy, Bingham, in 1585, under a scheme known as the Composition of Connaught. Thereby every man was to agree to pay 10s. per quarter of arable land per annum to his lord in lieu of the old erratic payments in service. The lord, in his turn, Norman and Irish alike, was to pay a fixed rent to the Government in Dublin. If one refuses to regard Irish history from any other standpoint than that of 'seven-hundred-years-of-slavery', if nothing is ever to be accepted as a *fait accompli* however unjust in its origins, whether the Danish, Norman, Tudor or Cromwellian colonizations, then it was, of course, another foul injustice to have thus exacted rent from Irishmen for their own native soil. The small farmers of Connaught seem to have been eager for the scheme and all historians are agreed that it was equitable.

One would, in any case, naturally expect that the common people would be the first to weary of the long and, to them, pointless struggle. They would have appreciated what the great Dan O'Connell, the emancipator of his people, said to an old man breaking stones by the road: 'Whatever happens, you will still be breaking stones.' The sixteenth-century English observers, at least, were quite satisfied, again not unnaturally, that 'the common Irish people have desired to leave their own lords and live under the English if they might'; and even claimed that these drudges were in favour of the Plantations that drove their chiefs to the bush:

they who live by their labours, and are yet hardly suffered by their unruly idle swordsmen to live in safety, or to enjoy of that which they get by their own labours, so much as to sustain their lives, expect to be relieved by the due execution of the laws . . .

Not that one accepts all such claims as facts, and the contemporary drudge the world over was probably no better off in his day. Nevertheless it is a fact that by the end of the sixteenth century the English seem to have had no difficulty in weaning away the poorer Irish from loyalty to their traditional chieftains. Of the great siege and battle of Kinsale (1601), which sounded the death-knell of the old Gaelic order, even so devoted a nationalist historian as Martin Haverty has to record with chagrin that one of the great disappointments of the Spaniards, who had come to Kinsale to help the Irish to overthrow the Protestant English yoke, was to find themselves besieged by an English army of up to 10,000 men strong, largely composed of Catholic Irish. The Lord President of Munster, Sir George Carew, had in his own personal army of 3,000 or so about 2,000 who were Irish. If this be true there must obviously have been something amiss with the rule of native chieftains who could not, in this hour of fate, command the loyalty of the common people. What was amiss is clear enough: ever since the Norman invasion the chieftains had become more and more feudal-minded, so that whenever they won back land from the Normans and their successors they did not treat it as tribal land but as personal property. The native upper classes were thus liked little better than nineteenth-century landlords.

There exists from the century following a most interesting document, a prose and verse satire in Gaelic called *The Parliament of Clan Thomas*, which throws a sharp light on what the upper classes of Gaelic society must have felt about the common folk from time immemorial, and were now to feel with an increasing bitterness as their own fortunes dwindled. The author or authors of this satire, evidently products of the old aristocratic bardic schools, adopt a form of heavy irony to flail the rising upstart 'boors', to wit, the common people. For within the sixty odd years between the Composition of Connaught, 1585, and 1650, when this satire was probably written, the old aristocratic world finally collapsed and the common people set themselves to make the best of the new world. The rise of all common folk is likely to be none too pleasant to watch. To leap forward yet once again we have seen the common folk of Ireland rise like the beanstalk out of the Revolution of 1922 and, for a generation, their behaviour was often very unpleasant to watch. In the seventeenth century, to use a vulgarism, the old aristocratic Gaelic order 'could not take it', and one finds it easy enough to sympathize with them.

In this satire the author invented a hateful ancestor for the rising 'boors', one Thomas, son of Putridpelt, son of Dragon-maggot, son of Beelzebub, and with ponderous sarcasm put into his mouth, and into the mouths of his bestial followers, every sort of revolutionary idea that the upper classes hated, such as that every member of Clan Thomas must set himself to plough – thus wiping out the old pastoral life on which Gaelic society had always been based; or, again, scornfully:

Cleave close together; populate farmsteads and townlands for yourselves; have neither lord nor master but your own selves; make the land dear for the nobility; put brown and red and blue on your clothes, wear collars and ruffs and gloves, and always use half-spurs, half-pillions and pommels.

The author's hate is evident in many passages.

They (the boors) spent their lives during the reign of every king, waiting on the nobles, in which manner they existed till the time of Elizabeth, daughter of Henry, the eighth king of that name, and during her reign they were in truth full of spunk and swelled head, pride and impudence, because of their abundant prosperity and plenty –

which takes us back directly to the date of the Composition of Connaught and indicates how much the Gaelic chiefs loathed its ordinances. Or there is this interesting passage, with its important four final words, summarizing the history of all the common folk from antiquity to those topsy-turvy days of the sixteenth and seventeenth century:

Clan Thomas spent their time merrily, well-fed and with light minds, as Saint Patrick had ordained for them. They did not [the author admits with satisfaction] use savoury succulent foods nor sweet intoxicating drinks, nor clean well-fitting clothes, but crude canvas shirts, slimy coarse swallow-tail coats woven of the foul hair of puck goats and other animals, stinking boots of untanned leather, crooked long-lappeted caps without make or shape, bedunged, bare, rusty, slippery clogs; while, as Patrick had bade them, they watched and waited, served and ploughed and slaved for the nobles and gentry of Christian kind during the reign of every king [he means every Gaelic king] from time immemorial, and they were craven before the kingly decrees, *as was their duty*.

It is, of course, just possible that this satire was composed in Swiftian terms, by somebody wholly in favour of the common people, but whatever its intention it marks a most important development in Irish social history – the first open breach between the ordinary peasant folk and the old native aristocracy, whom, one can only presume, they now thought of as failures.

There are other documents which indicate that the recriminations were mutual and savage.*

The occasion of this section, the fixed rent practice introduced by the Composition of Connaught, has at all times since been in the foreground of the peasant's mind. Over and over again from the seventeenth century on observers remark that if the tenant could pay his rent and live he counted himself a happy man. The thirst for security is, above all things, the great obsession of the peasant mind. And, in a long view, a deceptive obsession. The Irish tenants who compounded for a fixed rent in the sixteenth century won security and, in a sense, they won a degree of independence; but it was independence only of their chiefs' exactions, not a general independence as freemen. In the old system they were, as we have seen from our brief consideration of the Old Irish system, effectual freeholders: that is, they held their land, incontestably, for three generations at least. In the new system they were lease holders; that is, they held their land from year to year.

Now, if there is anything in English life to contrast with this change in the old Gaelic system it would be that which created the yeoman class, those who from 1430 onward were considered entitled to vote, i.e., farmers who worked their own freehold when it was worth forty shillings a year in the values of the time and who were known thereafter as the forty-shilling freeholders. (In the nineteenth century when at long last the vote was given to Irish Catholics only the forty-shilling freeholders were emancipated.) The old Gaelic-system 'farmer' had a vote, knew what it was and exercised it in elections. This new Irish farmer had no vote. He was a mere tenant, politically unfree, not a yeoman or freeman. And tenants – which, in Ireland, effectively speaking means 'peasants' – may have many wonderful and attractive qualities, and preserve valuable things in life, such as kindness, humour, charity, oral traditions, fellowship, a sense of wonder, even a sense of the magic of the world: but his virtues are always passive virtues, not the active virtues of initiative, direction, or invention. He will never, for

*The passages from *Clan Thomas* are quoted from translations in *The Bell* by Francis MacManus, beginning September 1943. A complete edition awaits publication.

example, contribute generative or revolutionary *ideas*. Thus, as Mr Christopher Dawson has pointed out to us, it was not the 'peasant' or tenant' spirit but the yeoman spirit which established English democracy, that tradition which kept alive there the sturdy English spirit of popular independence by never allowing the classes to get watertight. The yeoman and the burgesses have always been the stiffening in that prolonged fight for popular liberties, never the tenantry.

So it was with this first flicker of the rise of a tenant class in Ireland, which the old bardic aristocratic mind hated so furiously and understandably. Since we now know that they were, in time, to develop, under the leadership of the great Dan O'Connell, into the raw material of modern Irish democracy we can afford to welcome their arrival – we have no option, like the lady who said to Carlyle, 'I have decided to accept the universe'. But let us not be sentimental or romantic about them, and certainly not joyously enthusiastic in any kind of modern idealistic way, for theirs must have been for centuries a rather hopeless kind of mind, and they would never have arrived anywhere without the leadership of the townsmen. Even when O'Connell was leading them two hundred and fifty years later he cried that nobody would ever 'believe the species of *animals* with whom he had to carry on his warfare against the common enemy'. If this tenant mind has at last disappeared in Ireland it is mainly because almost all farmers are now freeholders. Having won not a short-term security but a long-term security, they are now as independent-minded as any yeoman, and as politically creative.

But all this is, I should stress, a wholly political or social comment. I have mentioned, and here again stress that the folk-mind is the repository of its own riches. It was not to the rich big farmers but to the poor men that Yeats went for the ancient memory which would seem to be their compensation on earth for their earthly misery. It is the poor and simple of heart who come closest to the gods, who cherish them long after they have been cast out elsewhere. The Irish 'peasant' is the child of time. He is its guardian and its slave. He will preserve for centuries dull and foolish habits that those who neither love nor fear time or change will quickly cast aside; but he will also preserve dear, ancient habits that like wine and ivory grow more beautiful and precious with age, all jumbled with the useless lumber in that dusty cockloft which is his ancestral mind.

The reformer, and the peasant is most often in the end his own reformer, foolishly takes a broom and sweeps it all out together in one heap like a ship discarding its ballast; and this seems to be inevitable, for he has no personal knowledge as to what is good or what is useless in his own ways, and knows only his ways, and if you change his ways you have taken the bottom out of his bag. When the poor, rent-paying peasant begins to live like a yeoman farmer his memory foreshortens: it is no longer an ancestral memory, it is merely a personal memory, which dies with him. In one generation folk can change into farmer – or into shopkeeper or civil servant for that matter. You then talk to him about 'the good people' and he will say, 'Ah, yes, I often remember when I was a young lad', or, 'I often remember my mother to do so and so', and it all means nothing to him because his life is no longer part of that ancient pattern. It is therefore futile to talk of reviving or of preserving the best rural ways unless one is also prepared to revive or retain the worst rural ways. And nobody on earth wants that, certainly nobody in Ireland, least of all the present-day planners whose whole ambition is to alter that rural way, to make it more and more scientific, profitable, comfortable and modern.

This makes a rather elementary remark necessary. Rural ways and the rural way persisted in Ireland longer and at a very much lower level than in Britain. It would be hard, for example, to imagine a book like George Sturt's *The Wheelwright's Shop* coming out of Ireland. Because of colonizations and wars and persecutions there is no *physical* continuity in Ireland like to the *physical* continuity in Britain, i.e. no ancient villages, with 'mossed cottage-trees', old inns, timbered houses, cropped greens, and handcrafts survive only in the simplest needs – turf-baskets, churns, farming implements, a few kitchen utensils.* We have, that is, an unfurnished countryside. Our racial memory is, it is true, very, very old; but in the foreground of it there is infinitely more of 'the ancient blinded vengeance

* See Estyn Evans, *The Irish Heritage* – as far as I know the only comprehensive book on this subject.

and the wrong that amendeth wrong' than there is of the happy life. Most of our physical embodiments of the past are ruins, as most of our songs are songs of lament and defiance. There is therefore far less reason here for the peasant to hang on to the rural way, or for the townsman to idealize it; when he does so it is always for what is called 'spiritual reasons'. The simplest illustration of all this is the fact that there is no Country Cult in Ireland – magazines appealing to the townsman's nostalgic dreams of life in the country – no *Countryside*, *Countryman*, *Country Life*. There is, simply, nowhere for people of civilized tastes to live in the country except in 'The Big House', and the latest census returns show that even the country people themselves are still drifting rapidly towards the towns. So, on the one hand modern Ireland is striving hard to catch 'up' with the rest of the world in industry and business, and must strive, on the other hand, to build an attractive country life – on very little foundation – to keep her young people in the fields.

All this is far removed from our Connaught tenant-farmer of 1585, the first date at which we can identify him as holding a recognizable legal position in the social system. Sir Richard Bingham had no idea of creating what Euripides calls 'the men who alone save a nation'; and later upheavals were, in any case, so to persecute and depress the peasantry that their work in 'saving the nation' was to be, even in the agrarian struggle of the nineteenth century, politically-orientated rather than socially-orientated. The date is, none the less, another finger-post in that direction. In our day history seems to be writing yet another – the peasant, after many vicissitudes, entering into possession of a town life which was made for him, in its beginnings, by Dane, Norman, Tudor and Anglo-Irish. Here he seems to be fumbling in an ungainly fashion with strange tools, rather lost, not very attractive, developing into a bastard type which is neither countryman nor townsman, unable, as yet to make a smooth transition from the simplicity of the fields to the sophistication of the streets.

It is too soon, yet, to say what the inscription on this finger-post may finally be, what the 'peasant' may do with the inheritance of a history formed mainly under rural conditions now that, as in so many other countries, he is becoming subject to a widespread process of urbanization. But as I look back to the Ireland of my youth, which means to look back to the years before and during the First World War, I see an enormous change for the better. Fifty years ago the average country town, for example, was still very much as described by Thackeray or Charles Lever – muddy, unkempt, uncouth, unhealthy, miserably isolated and virtually devoid of any normal civil amenities. Even as recently as the mid-twenties when I happened to spend a year as a teacher in a typical country town in Clare, with a population of 6,000 or so, there was no bus service, no library, no cinema, no dance hall, no really good hotel, no café. I cannot remember anybody possessing a radio, and television had not yet come. Today that town has all those things, including a first-class hotel. Roadside lounge bars and even motels are growing. Even in the smallest villages today one may come on a café, generally tolerable, occasionally with some such ambitious name like *La Bonne Bouche*. Cars being widespread nobody feels cut off. As for rural travel fifty years ago it was often like travelling in Calabria in the days of Norman Douglas. Today, roads are good almost everywhere. One of the most welcome of modern developments is the appearance of the farm Guest House, fostered by the Tourist Board, which insists on baths, hot and cold water, comfortable beds, electricity (except in remote places like the Aran Islands), absolute cleanliness and good plain cooking. Such an amenity was unthinkable in my youth. There are, of course, corresponding losses. Most rural crafts are vanishing, as for instance buttermaking; most folk ways and old beliefs are abraded; many simple pleasures and even country sports are on the way out. Who now ambles around the country in the old pony-trap? Even to find horse-riding is not easy. The roadside dance-board is a thing of the past.

Aesthetically one must regret the change over from the old thatched cottage to the modern, healthier but rather unlovely tiled bungalow; one may even regret the change from coloured shawls and red petticoats to modern mass-produced dresses. It is all part of the price one has to pay for modernization.

Any people [says Margaret Mead] will produce a beautiful homogeneous aesthetic if you leave them stagnant long enough. Even their pots and pans will fit their cottages. And if they have had very few pots and pans, and haven't invented a new one for five hundred years you can be sure everything fits. In our society nothing fits anything else. Aesthetically every society that changes is thoroughly unsatisfactory.

In Ireland, as elsewhere from New Guinea to old Glencolumcill, those three great blessings and curses of modern life, the internal combustion engine, the telephone, and television have telescoped the process of change just a bit too fast for men (and women) to keep pace with it. It is, however, probably only the older generation that notices the loss of tradition incurred – and even they only intermittently, at the jog of memory when returning to the scenes of their youth.

9

THE ANGLO-IRISH

THE last stand of the old Gaelic aristocracy in the sixteenth century, was conducted by a very great man indeed, Hugh O'Neill, Earl of Tyrone, and if anybody could have pulled the fractionalism of Ireland together he would have done it. But it is not necessary for us to delay over Tyrone's magnificent effort to save the Gaelic world from itself because we are already familiar with all its inherent weaknesses which appear the more exasperating at the end only because Tyrone deserved better than to have had to cope with them.

In my biography of Tyrone* I have drawn all the usual conclusions, but one more occurs to me in this context. Tyrone had been reared as a child in England; he was one of the shrewdest men in the Europe of his day; he behaved all through his life as one who knows two worlds and can live at will in either; effectively, he was an Irish feudal baron of the greatest power, greater than any Norman baron had ever been, more powerful than Strongbow, or the Red Earl, or Ormond, or Desmond. In England, he would have been of the timber of kingmaker, and perhaps even of king. He could not have won in Ireland because his human material was not feudal. *Nobody* could have welded the Irish chiefs, except by hammering their proud heads together – and they would have returned joyously to their old suicidal ways immediately their dictator died.

The date of the defeat of Tyrone by Mountjoy, before his flight to the Continent, where he was received with the greatest honour and lodged in luxury in Rome by the Pope until his death, was 1603. That year is the great death-gong of Irish history, echoing back and back into the hollow halls of the Celtic world, mingling with the groans and sighs of a score of cursing kings who, like him, were thrown and trampled by the wild Irish mustangs. It echoes forward, for three hundred years, in

*The Great O'Neill, London, 1942.

tones of regret that grow ever softer and sweeter as the memory blurs until, by the end, one might almost think that this was Elysium and the Hesperides and Olympus and Arcadia all in one that the last poor, outcast Gaelic poetasters kept on be-wailing and eulogizing: though, in truth, it *had* been an Ar-cadia for them – if for no one else. Even the new peasantry, whose arrival we have marked, were doubtless so foolish at times as to bewail it too.

Only one positive and creative thing came out of the last wreck of Gaeldom: Ulster as we now know it. O'Neill was an Ulster chief, and on his fall his territory was planted by English and Lowland Scots, mainly Presbyterian, but not wholly: the first Earl of Antrim was a Highlander and a Catholic. Many of the old Gaelic families remained on for a time in Ulster; few were to survive Cromwell. It was, as usual, only the small men who survived. They bowed to the storm; their standards were poor; they could be hired cheaply:

It was not until after 1660 that the Scottish element in Ulster be-came a pronounced success and is the only case of a real, democratic, industrial and labouring colony established in Ireland. Ulster finally became a province almost entirely Protestant as regards the land-owners and mainly so as regards the population, and it is reckoned that in 1641 of the three and a half million acres in the Six Counties the Protestants owned three million and the Catholics the rest. But even this proportion was to be reduced after 1660, and after 1690 scarcely anything of the Gaelic and Catholic aristocracy remained.*

This vast Plantation is the origin of Ireland's modern Parti-tion problem; for, interspersed with these colonists in the north-east, a Catholic and Irish minority in the whole Province has tenaciously persisted to this day. Partition is their tragedy. For the moment we may be content to observe this new, wholesale blending of fresh blood, this intrusion of another new men-tality, and remember that still more plantations followed under James and Charles, in Wexford, Carlow and Wicklow, and there were wholesale clearances under Cromwell. So, in a county like Carlow one must expect today dominant twists of Gaelic, Norman and seventeenth-century Protestant settlers, all now

* Curtis, *History of Ireland*, p. 232.

inextricably mingled with lesser healthy infusions unnoticed by any other histories than the parish records.

All through the seventeenth century, then, the old aristocratic Gaelic world was dying of the death-blow of 1603. It was in one sense a life-blow, a blow in the face that made the country awaken, though too late, far far too late, from its long somnambulism – or if not 'the country' in any modern connotation, at any rate a greater coherence of Irishmen than had ever been possible before. Twice in the seventeenth century one can almost point, at last, to a politically national mind – in the two great upheavals of the Insurrection of 1641 and the Jacobite Wars that came to a close with the Battle of the Boyne (1690) and the Siege of Limerick (1691). Irishmen of every class and origin took part in these wars, some fighting for religion, some for land, some for Charles I or James II, some for the old Gaelic traditional life-mode, some for an independent native parliament, some against this minor grievance, some against that: and although we note that neither of these wars was fought for what the modern vocabulary would call 'Irish Independence' – and it was no longer conceivable that any coherent fight could be raised for any simple slogan – yet these wars of the seventeenth century show one considerable development in Irish thought: men were at last beginning to think in terms of mutual accommodation, were learning that society is a complex, and often a dissidence, and that there are techniques to bring this syncretism to a synthesis. Their tardy efforts failed, but the experience cannot have been wholly loss.

Out of this country in which the old aristocracy fell a new aristocracy began to emerge. It was almost wholly new, but not entirely so. True, the 'old English', mainly Norman, gentry went down at the Boyne with the last peerages of Gaelic blood – such as Iveagh and Clancarty. But enough of these 'old English' remained to hand on distinctively Irish ways and traditions to this Protestant and Anglican ascendancy that developed out of the plantations of James I and Cromwell. As J. M. Hone has pointed out, Bishop Berkeley (1685–1753), whose family had been only one generation in Ireland, could proudly write at the close of his polemic against Newton: 'We Irish think otherwise'; and the two great Protestant defenders of Irish political rights in the eighteenth century, Swift and Molyneux, were sympathetic to many purely native traditions, the one praising the Catholic gentry defeated at the Boyne, the other taking a lively interest in the Gaelic language. This new ascendancy or aristocracy of the seventeenth century is what we call today the 'Anglo-Irish'. They were to bring to Ireland a greater concentration of civil gifts than any previous, or later, colonizers: one may, indeed, be done with it in one sentence by saying that culturally speaking the Anglo-Irish were to create modern Irish-thinking, English-speaking, English-writing Ireland. Politically, and in the largest sense socially, they were either wicked, indifferent, or sheer failures.

The heyday of this Anglo-Irish enclave was the eighteenth century; their nearest-to-hand monument is Dublin's grace, roominess, magnificence and unique atmosphere; but all about the country they built gracious houses (each to be known to the native tenantry as 'The Big House') and pleasant seats, such as Castletown, near Dublin (1716) or Rockingham, near Boyle, County Roscommon (1810), which are the epitome of the classical spirit of that cultured and callous century. They were, however, a separate enclave. They resided in Ireland – their country, never their nation – so that their achievements were, for the most part, so remote from the life of the native Irish (now utterly suppressed) that they ultimately became part of the English rather than the Irish cultural record. Goldsmith and Burke are obvious examples.

However, as we may see in the next chapter, the Anglo-Irish were far from being altogether an alien and detached strain in Irish life. One need only mention such names as Lord Edward Fitzgerald, or Robert Emmet, or Thomas Davis, or Parnell to show at once that this is so. One may see from the example of letters alone how active their interest was, how intimate and how fructive. From the famous Protestant Archbishop James Ussher (d. 1656), or English Sir James Ware (d. 1666) to Charlotte Brooke (d. 1793) or Charles Vallancey, an Englishman of French Protestant parentage (d. 1812), many of the new ascendancy worked, in selfless devotion in generation after generation, side by side with native Irishmen, to preserve the traditions, language and history of Ireland. These men, and they were legion, were the unwitting forerunners of the modern popular Gaelic revival, whose founder, Douglas Hyde, (first President of Ireland) was himself an Anglo-Irishman of the Protestant faith.

What the Normans had done was to bring the vigour of their own, foreign, culture to bear on a decaying native culture. Their gifts were social, political and military. As we have seen the chief thing they did was to help to urbanize a pastoral people. The Anglo-Irish continued this urbanization. All the planned aspects of the prettier villages and towns in Ireland are their handiwork – Westport, Lismore, Midleton, Youghal, Kinsale, the eighteenth-century parts of Cork and Limerick, small villages like Adare or Enniskerry, the quays of Clonmel, the pleasant bits of Carlow and Kilkenny, Wexford and Birr: in every Irish county they have left this welcome mark. I speak of it, however, not so much to indicate a further gift as to introduce the basic dichotomy. How often do we not meet on the edges of Irish towns, usually on the edge nearest the hinterland, a suburb known as 'Irishtown'. (See, for example, the Irishtown of Kilkenny, divided from the central town by a small – now concealed – river.) The barrier, that is to say, which originally existed between Normans and Gaels, and which was in the end worn away, was erected again by the Anglo-Irish, conveniently symbolized for us by these Irishtowns; or by those long, winding demesne walls which still so tiresomely blot out the scenery for the traveller.

The barrier which was to prove the most formidable of all was the difference in religion. The Normans were Catholics. The Anglo-Irish were Protestants or Anglicans. (Some of them are touchy about being called 'non-Catholics' and Catholics so dislike the political connotations of Protestantism that, in mistaken delicacy, they think it milder to call them non-Catholics.) The outward symbol of that barrier is the Catholic church relegated to a remote or back street (cheaper ground, also less likely to attract attention) and the Protestant church plumb in the middle of a town square, or on the hill: and one will note how often the Catholic church is without a spire – that little arrogance forbidden by law. Thus in my native city of Cork the great trident of the spires of the Protestant Cathedral dominates the city, all the older Catholic churches are hidden away, and none has a spire. These things remind us that one of the most cultivated and creative societies in western Europe during the eighteenth century was also politically barbarous.

And now for the solution of this dichotomy. The century was not without a conscience – noble-minded men who loathed the injustices they saw on all sides, and in the Dublin Parliament strained to alleviate them. These were the 'Patriot Party' reviving the old Norman claims to autonomy in terms of a new Protestant nationalism. They fought local corruption, British interference, demanded Free Trade, control of revenue, sought to relieve the Catholic masses from the worst of their local disabilities, even while, on the other hand, they had no plan for any organic change in the social system and kept their tenantry in a condition so beastly that Chesterfield thought them treated worse than Negro slaves.

The Patriot Party's real gift to the native Irish was a political lesson which was to dominate the popular imagination for the next hundred and forty years. They seized on the foreign troubles of England, in America, France, Spain, and Holland, to found an armed force of Protestant Volunteers, originally and ostensibly to defend the country against invasion, ultimately and ostentatiously to win the absolute independence of the Irish Parliament; which they did in 1782. True, this bloodless revolt proved abortive; firstly, because the Parliament represented only the Anglo-Irish enclave, and could not gather up enough vision or courage to give the vote to the Roman Catholic majority, and secondly, because in 1800 – two years after the native Irish, at last driven to desperation, had risen in rebellion – the Dublin Parliament was completely abolished by Pitt. The memory of these Volunteers gave to the masses the famous motto, 'England's difficulty is Ireland's opportunity', with its implied reliance on physical force and its evident despair of all constitutional techniques. Above all, as we must next see by going back a few years to 1791, this armed defiance of the Patriot Party created a new Irish type, the Rebel, in whom native Irish and Anglo-Irish became and have ever since found the personification of a single-minded nationalism.

10

THE REBELS

In 1791, in Belfast, that house built upon a house, among the Presbyterian Dissenters, there was founded a secret society known as The United Irishmen aiming at a 'brotherhood of affection and a communion of rights and a union of power among Irishmen of every religious persuasion'. The source of this generative idea was France. I have earlier quoted W. P. Ker on the old Celtic mind and its literature to intimate that its struggle was towards intellectual and imaginative freedom. We have seen in that literature one or two abortive adventures of the racial kind groping for this freedom. It is striking that, in the end, it is not in culture but in politics, not in Gaelic Ireland but in Anglo-Ireland, not among Catholics but Nonconformists that the fog suddenly lifts on a bit of clear-cut logic. But no word must be said that would suggest for a moment a cold or abstract mind. The chief figure of the United Irishmen was a man of charming personality, merry wit, and civilized ideas about life in general. He had had noble precursors and contemporaries – Swift is an example of the one and Grattan of the other – but, to steal the words of a famous password about another amiable Irishman, 'Wolfe Tone is the name and Wolfe Tone is the man'. This young Protestant Dubliner, educated at Trinity College, that alien nursery of native causes, was to unite the logic of the northern Scot to the passions of the southern Irish, to scatter the timidities of the peasants and the vacillations of the tradesmen with his vision of the new revolutionary age. In Tone's hands the French Revolution became a trumpet, unheard indeed by the dust of antiquity, and one can only laugh to think what the bardic caste would have said of him; heard by only a small number of the millions of slaves about him, but heard by enough men to have handed down to our day a gay and passionate republican spirit that is never likely to die wholly in Ireland.

The cleavage with the past is immense. A century before and the fumes of a thousand years were still lingering about us. Almost without warning Wolfe Tone flings open the doors of the modern world like a thunderclap. Nothing less dramatic can describe a change so great as to see Jacobin ideas spreading, at whatever highly simplified remove from their original form, among a Gaelic-speaking peasantry.

This combination of what one must call a controlled Anglo-Irish intelligence and a passionate sense of injustice among the native Irish – in so far as there was by now any blood unmixed enough to be called 'native Irish' – is the formula of modern Irish nationalism. Tone, Parnell and Griffith are examples. The common people burned with a sense of their undeniable wrongs; the new middle classes, of whatever religion, found their country – or the country of their adoption – being misruled by an utterly corrupt, inefficient and pandering Parliament in the selfish interests of Britain. But the peasantry had no ideas and the middle classes had no force. The peasantry did, indeed, form into secret violent societies (The Whiteboys and Shanavests and so forth) to revenge themselves on local tyrants; and for the enlargement or sublimation of their hates and hopes could still listen to the wandering Gaelic poets weaving Vision Poems, or *Aislingi*, in which the ancient world was once again restored by the Stuarts returning in triumph from France or Spain. But neither these impossible dreams nor those sporadic outbursts could be of much help except as a heady drink may keep up a poor devil's spirits until his real chance arrives.

Neither could the timid methods of the Catholic Whiggish middle classes achieve much by loyal addresses since they were content to accept the current social order provided they could remove the restrictions under which their own class suffered: they were otherwise indifferent to the real canker of their country, i.e. the hideous economic slavery in which the masses of the people existed as mere cottiers without rights, without security, without a vote, without hope. It was from the top alone, from the free-minded intellectuals, such as Tone, and from the more humane aristocrats of the new Anglo-Irish order that a fighting leadership could come. Since, in the end, the aristocracy was subject to the corruption of its own vested interests, which not even the devotion of Grattan and his Patriot Party could hold at bay, that leadership of the people devolved in the end on the intellectuals.* They became the interpreters of the new America and the new France. Thanks to their propaganda the vacuum left in the Irish mind by the fall of the Norman and Gaelic aristocracy was filled by the most explosive ideas of modern democratic Europe.

Things have so much changed since that century, there are now so many other quarters from which leadership might at any moment emerge for a national agitation – the Church, the writers, the Labour movement, our political parties, the Press – that we must emphasize this isolation of Tone and his companions in the Ireland of the 1790s. I have mentioned five modern alternatives; obviously the last four did not then exist. We must see, too, why the Catholic Church was to all intents and purposes wholly supine at this period.

It was not until the first decade of the following century that any signs of spirit appear among the Catholic clergy, and then a man like the famous 'J.K.L.', James Warren Doyle, Bishop of Kildare and Leighlin, forms an astonishing contrast not only to his predecessors but even to his contemporaries. This is not surprising. We remember that for generations the official – and legal – title for a Catholic was 'Papist'; that the Catholic Church was never referred to as such but as 'the Roman Catholic communion in Ireland', as if it were a peculiar local sect; that priests generally dressed in discreet brown so as not to attract attention and are always (as in Tone's diaries) spoken of as 'Mister' So-and-so; that an Archbishop of Dublin, in forwarding a curate's letter to Dublin Castle for perusal, could humbly add, 'You note he calls me "Lord", but I do not claim the title, and I can't prevent him from using it'; that, as Tom Moore noted in his diary, whereas Archbishop Troy, the Catholic, died worth tenpence, the Protestant Archbishop of Armagh left

* It was not, in fact, until Tone and his comrades expelled the tame Catholic aristocrats from their committees that they won, by the Relief Act of 1793, the removal of the major disabilities under which Catholics had suffered since Limerick and the Boyne, e.g., they could carry a gun, go to Dublin University (Protestant – the only University), vote as forty-shilling freeholders in the counties, hold minor offices, act as grand jurors, take commissions in the army.

£130,000, having throughout his life enjoyed an income of
£20,000 a year, largely made up of the pence of peasants (Catholics) unwillingly subscribed as tithes. It sums up the dispirited-
ness of the Catholic Church that when Dr Doyle became Bishop
– Tone then seventeen years dead – he found that nobody had
dared hold a confirmation service in his diocese for twenty
years, his chapels were thatched cabins, the vestments were
worn and torn, the sacred chalices were old or even leaked.

'J.K.L.' did, in his day, give magnificent encouragement to
his people. On the other hand he was a rigid constitutionalist:
his great opponents were the secret societies that the rebelly
spirit of the century before had set flourishing among the tough
men of the collieries, and he fought them to his dying day –
often literally with the sweat pouring off him, haranguing them
in their basalt thousands under the open sky. This horror of
physical revolt, of all revolutionary defiance for established law
and order – a horror often felt by the people as a betrayal of
their cause – goes so deep into the repressive spirit of the Church
of the time that it is worth probing a little farther into the causes
of it, and its prolonged effects.

As we know, the great Catholic seminary of Maynooth was
founded, long before Catholic emancipation, even before the
1798 Rebellion, out of British Government funds. We need
not inquire whether the Government hoped to purchase the
loyalty of the Church; for though it certainly got it, that was
because of chance circumstances that it could not have foreseen. In 1795, the year of Maynooth's foundation, there were a
great many French refugee professors and teachers to whom
any haven, the most frugal pension, would have been welcome.
This suited Maynooth perfectly, for it was not a rich foundation,
and, as one may imagine, Ireland (just emerging from the Penal
Code) was in no position to supply it with sufficient native
scholars. It gave posts to several of these distinguished men,
such as Delahogue and Anglade for moral and dogmatic theology, thereby importing a French school of thought whose teachings so carefully, indeed fanatically, cultivated the spirit of
Gallicanism among the Irish clergy that the Irish Church soon
became Gallican to the core, and remained so for nearly half a
century.

That is: in politics, through their hatred of the Revolutionary spirit, in their devotion to the old monarchical absolutism, they filled the mind of most Irish priests, all through O'Connell's great fight against Britain, with the traditional Gallican belief that all things, even many of the privileges of the Church, must lie in servile subjection to the throne; and, in morals, they encouraged a repulsive rigour in the management of consciences which rendered the following of Christ's teachings anything but a *jugum suave*. They proscribed many of the classic theologians of the Church, such as Suarez or Molina, both Jesuits, the first of whom had written against the Oath of Allegiance to the crown, the second of whom had humanely tried to reconcile free-will and predestination. Liguori, even after his beatification, was not safe from the censure of those bitter French exclusivists at Maynooth – one actually told his students that the saint was *perdite laxus*. They were so far from all accommodativeness, benignity, mildness, so far from trying to make the Law easier for the people, that one of the prevailing class-books at Maynooth, that of Bailly, had to be put on the Papal Index in 1852.

An alien theology possessing for us neither national nor other interests thus balefully affected the youth and manhood of the Irish Church, narrowing their views, misdirecting their professional studies and if not entirely estranging their feelings of allegiance at least sensibly weakening them towards the true object of Catholic loyalty.

When this mentality was finally exorcised from Maynooth I do not know; its full, hateful rigour cannot have outlasted the 1850s there – but it had by then been carried through the length and breadth of Ireland by priests educated under the old régime, and when a sharp controversy (from which I take the last quotation) developed in 1879 over a sudden lifting of the veil by Dr Henry Neville, Rector of the Catholic University, ex-professor of Maynooth, one of the reasons why his would-be refuter (Dr Walsh, later Archbishop Walsh; d. 1921) was angry with him was that so many priests who had passed through the College in the epoch under question were still working among the people – and training their young curates according to their own ideas.

A tradition like that eddies on. Even in our day readers of

Canon Sheehan's excellent novel, *The Blindness of Doctor Gray*, will recognize a familiar priest of the old school, the stern moralist for whom 'The Law' was a second god. In my youth this rigorous priest was a commonplace, 'the man with the blackthorn stick', scouring the hedges at night to beat the lovers, thundering from the pulpit about the immorality of what was then known as V necks (on girls' blouses), and silk stockings. Any man or woman who married a Protestant was as good as damned. Any Catholic who attended a Protestant funeral or marriage was sent direct to the Bishop of his diocese for forgiveness. One meets this priest constantly in the political and clerical history of the nineteenth century, as in 'J.K.L.'s' disagreements even with Delahogue and Anglade (see Fitzpatrick's *Life*, pp. 83, 156), MacHale's with O'Finian (O'Reilly's *Life*, I, p. 345), or again in Doyle's brush with the Jesuits at Clongowes (op. cit., p. 142) whom he tried to *stop* from hearing confessions because he thought them too lenient! And, of course, as we know, both Doyle and MacHale were anti-Republican because of their youthful experiences, the latter in Ireland, the former in Portugal when Napoleon invaded it in 1807. Doyle stood sentry at Coimbra during those exciting months, and went to Lisbon to act as interpreter for the English under that other famous Irishman, Wellesley. But if one grasps this key one understands a lot of things much better, especially why it was that O'Connell had to fight not merely the British but his own bishops, the English and Irish Catholic aristocrats, and even defy Rome herself in the famous Veto question, i.e., the 'right' of the Crown to hand-pick Ireland's Bishops. This was the occasion of O'Connell's famous *pronunciamentos* that if the Catholics of Ireland must accept the order of Pius VII to accept royal nomination of their own bishops he would, in future, rather take his politics from Constantinople than from Rome, and that such bishops would, in fact, be the means of uncatholicizing the land.* One understands best of all what a

---

* It sums up the period, 1805–45, to say that O'Connellism in the presbytery was fighting, and defeating, Gallicanism in the seminary. Long before O'Connell there were, of course, noble exceptions among the priesthood: one has only to recall the priests who died with the gun in their hands in 1798, or who were hanged or shot after the Rising ended.

task poor Tone had, way back in the 1790s, to rouse the Catholic laity and priesthood.

The masses, then, had no other fighting leaders but Tone and the United Irishmen in the 1790s; and these were trying to build up a new mentality, a new mind, against every opposition, lay and clerical. Of that new mind Tone, first and before all others, is the personification. That was his main contribution, to give to his people the dynamism of his own nature, the example of his own life. Overtly he and the United Irishmen were to achieve, directly or indirectly, very little: the bloody Rising of 1798, a failure; two abortive efforts to invade Ireland from France; a brief rising in the west. But he was to sow ideas broadcast. He was to present common men with their first personal hero of the new democratic age. He was to leave behind him a diary in which his merry, insuppressible, eager, all too human nature, so sceptical, so serious, so gay, so indiscreet, so utterly removed from all posing or false dignity, is a happy definition not merely of the man but of his ideals. It and he are the only sensible definition that exists of what a sadly decreasing number of Irishmen mean today when they talk of being Republicans. He was to become the beau-ideal of Irish rebels, the great prototype on which all later would-be revolutionaries instinctively modelled themselves.

This rebel mentality has become so rooted in Ireland and has so coloured all our other characteristics, and so profoundly affected our social behaviour, our symbolism, our literature, even our conventions, that we should strive hard to understand it. Irishmen themselves possibly understand it least of all since with them it is not so much a question of understanding as of the discussion of something too familiar even to propose self-questions.

The rebel seems to fall into two types or stages. The first rebels against an immediate injustice – peasant risings follow, peasant societies of revenge, workers' associations. He sees no farther. The other sees beyond the immediate thing to the larger implications: he is the man who uses words like Emancipation, Liberty, Freedom. The one is clear as to his object; the other is never clear. He cannot be because his desirable image of life is not something which forms in a vacuum but something whose instruments are flesh and blood. He is subject to the limitations of his followers and times. This intellectual type of rebel is always the national leader, as against the local leader, and it is his dilemma that, in the ultimate, he is leading people to a Promised Land which *they*, not he, must define and create. He is riding a raft on a swirling river, and like all leaders of masses of men it may well be his constant problem whether he is riding the torrent or the torrent is driving him.

The Rebel was devoted to failure. He was a professional or vocational failure. Not that he did not dream of and hope for success. But he always knew the odds were against him and if he was a Wolfe Tone, laughed cheerfully at his possible, indeed probable, fate. (Tone joked over the usual fate of his kind – to be hanged and disembowelled – 'A fig for the disembowelling if they hang me first.') There was only one thing at which the Rebel wished to be a success and that was at rebelling. Death did not mean failure so long as the Spirit of Revolt lived. The Rebel did not even mind obliteration and anonymity, and thousands upon thousands of Irish rebels have never been recorded and their sacrifice will never be known.

Nor are Irish rebels peculiar in this. One of the most eloquent tributes ever paid to anonymous sacrifice occurs in that remarkable, and too little known, English novel, *The Revolution in Tanner's Lane*, by Mark Rutherford. I think it worth giving here in full:

To work hard for those who will thank us, to head a majority against oppressors is a brave thing but far more honour is due to [those] who strove for thirty years from the outbreak of the French Revolution onwards not merely to rend the chains of the prisoners, but had to achieve the far more difficult task of convincing them that they would be happier if they were free. These heroes are forgotten or nearly so. Who remembers the poor creatures who met in the early mornings on the Lancashire moors or were shot by the yeomanry? They sleep in graves over which stands no tombstone, or probably their bodies have been carted away to make room for a railway which has been driven through their last resting-place. They saw the truth before those whom the world delights to honour as its political redeemers; but they have perished utterly from our recollection and will never be mentioned in history. Will there ever be a great Day of Assize when a just judgement shall be pronounced;

when all the impostors who have been crowned for what they did not deserve will be stripped, and the Divine word will be heard calling upon the faithful to inherit the Kingdom, – who, when 'I was anhungered gave me meat, when I was thirsty gave me drink; when I was a stranger took me in; when I was naked visited me; when I was in prison came unto me'? Never! It was a dream of an enthusiastic Galilean youth, and let us not desire that it may ever come true. Let us rather gladly consent to be crushed into indistinguishable dust, with no hope of record: rejoicing only if some infinitesimal portion of the good work may be achieved by our obliteration, and content to be remembered only in that anthem which in the future it will be ordained shall be sung in our religious services in honour of all holy apostles and martyrs who have left no name.

Even of those who are recorded, honoured and well known what *is* known clearly? The one thing about them which is always clear is their personalities. Thus, what Tone would have done had he been first President of an Irish Republic nobody knows, because he has not told us. But from the nature of the man we can see the kind of life that would have pleased him, and the things (for example) in modern Ireland that he would not have tolerated, such as the least sign of sectarianism, puritanism, middle-class vulgarity, canting pietism, narrow orthodoxies whether of Church or State. One feels that his laughter and his humanity would have blown all these away, would have defined political liberty not merely in terms of comfort but of gaiety and tolerance and a great pity and a free mind and a free heart and a full life. And if few rebels have been so gay as Tone, except perhaps in our own time Mick Collins, wherever the Rebel appears he will always reveal the same composition – even the most solemn and subjective of them, such as Pearse – or else he is a faux-rebel or a lapsed-rebel, that most common and pathetic type in the history of all peoples.

The thing could not have been otherwise. Rebelly Wolfe Tone was doomed to leave so little behind him, to be unclear in his ideas, to be fuddled even, to be a failure, because he chose to lock-knit himself with the common people, with the poorest and most ignorant of his countrymen whose whole lives, day after day, were themselves the very epitome of befuddlement and failure. He was not their tutor: he was their torch, their friend, their lover. He went down into the huts and cabins and took the people to his heart. He was not telling them about their future – they had no future. He was telling them about their present – about themselves. He was their second priest. It was rebels like him whom in turn the poor have always loved with an unbreakable loyalty, made ballads about them, hung their likenesses in cheap pictures about their walls, revered as their symbols – Tone, Emmet, Lord Edward, Napper Tandy, O'Connell, Mitchel, Parnell and all the rebels of 1916 and after.

This is not to detract from those other Irishmen who, in their humanity, kindness and sensibility, contributed throughout the nineteenth century to the spirit of liberalism, but who pledged their minds to success in the sense that as gradualists they were satisfied to win reform little by little, and to clear-sightedness in the sense that they would not look beyond those immediate and possible goals. These were our pure constitutionalists like that devoted and patriotic first leader of the Irish Party, Isaac Butt, and its last leader John Redmond, and there were earlier men, like John Keogh, and hundreds of others earlier and later still, and doubtless there always will be, whose natural sense of decencies ranges them, though at a remove of prudence or qualified disapproval, on the side of (if not beside) the rebelly-minded.

A good example of these men was O'Connell's lieutenant O'Neill Daunt whose autobiography, well-named *A Life Spent for Ireland*, loyally veils but does not conceal his distaste for O'Connell's brash techniques. But just as it is quite evident that O'Neill Daunt could never have accomplished what O'Connell accomplished by his rumbustious, indeed often, if not always, slightly vulgar, flamboyant defiance, his – call it if one wills tricky or even dishonest – methods of inflaming the people to the very edge of open revolt, and as in the Tithe War well beyond it, in short by his use of the rebel-mind in thought and action, so never once, I dare say, did any constitutionalist win one of those gradual reforms without the Rebel as the real force behind him.

This is illustrated over and over during the hundred years after Tone. It is that century in a nutshell. Tone died in 1798. O'Connell was at work from 1807. The next rebel movement, the Young Irelanders, began in 1842 and broke into armed revolt on his death. Ten years later Fenianism began under Stephens and O'Donovan Rossa, and there were attempted outbreaks in 1865 and 1867. That 'life and death question' of Ireland in the nineteenth century, land trouble – which had scattered violence all over the country ever since O'Connell's day with its inevitable aftermaths of evictions and emigrations – was boiling ever since 1852, and was to be the centre of the Parnellite campaign. Interwoven with all this was the constitutional effort. Isaac Butt, to lead the Irish Party from 1870 on, defended the Fenians in 1865. Parnell was converted to Nationalism by the execution of the three Irish Fenians who attempted the famous prison release in Manchester in 1867. The first of a series of Land Acts that were, ultimately, to change the whole character of the peasantry, namely Gladstone's Act of 1870, came out of violence and murder in Tipperary. The Land Bill of 1881, which at last fixed the tenant's rent and prevented landlords from practising any longer that brutal and ambition-destroying trick of increasing the rent whenever a tenant by his own industry improved his holding, came out of one of the most violent periods of Davitt's Land League agitation. And so on.

If there is in all this a distinction between the 'common people' and others who are not 'the people' I can only say *circumspice*. That is the way the story has gone. I say it in no spirit of democratic enthusiasm for the 'common people' who are, to the artist and the intellectual, so often a bore and an aggravation, whose lives and minds are most creative and interesting when they themselves are most poor and least emancipated, as when Yeats 'discovered' them, still a traditional peasantry.

What was it that the Irish Rebel always sacrificed? The better part of his life? Far worse, far more exhausting, harder far to bear, he sacrificed the better part of his mind. Men like Tone, Mitchel, Doheny, all of them, had smothered talents. They were presumably men with as much human ambition as anybody else, and more sensibility than most. It was a drudge to them to 'go down into the cabins of the people'. How bored Tone was by these talks and meals with dithering, half-educated Catholic tradesmen and farmers; and he was the last man to whine or complain. 'Cowardly enough.' 'A dirty personal jealousy.' 'Our mob, very shabby fellows.' 'Shabby.' 'A blockhead, without parts or principles.' 'The parish priest, a sad vulgar booby.' 'Egan of Galway is flinching.' 'Sick.' 'Victuals bad, wine poisonous, bed execrable.' 'Sad, sad.' 'Dinner with the Catholics, dull as ten thousand devils. Dismal, dreary.' 'Damn them, ignorant bigots' (this about two Catholic bishops). 'Gog (this is John Keogh, the most pious of Catholics and most devoted, though timid) tells me he begins to see the Catholic bishops are all scoundrels.' 'Cowardly! Cowardly!' (this about men who are trying to dodge taking the chair at a meeting). And so it goes on. But how even that far tougher metal, the great and burly Dan O'Connell, used to curse those 'common people' as when he called them 'animals', and 'crawling slaves'!

All these men deprived themselves, and Ireland, of as much as they gave: they choked the critical side of their minds, they were good rebels in proportion as they were bad revolutionaries. Their passion for change and their vision of change never pierced to organic change, halted dead at the purely modal and circumstantial. It had to be that way since they devoted their lives and all their beings to passion rather than to thought, or in Arnold's words describing the French Revolution 'had their source in a great movement of feeling, not in a great movement of mind'. Not that Arnold's ideas in the first of his *Essays in Criticism* have any political validity, and certainly no validity as between Ireland and England since (as he recognizes freely, certainly by implication throughout) you might as well have tried to change an Englishman's political views about his Empire by reasoning with him as hope to stop the charge of an elephant with an epigram. And, furthermore, as Arnold also agrees, though so subtly as to gloss over the inherent contradiction, the French Revolution

undoubtedly found its motive-power in the intelligence of men. . . . The French Revolution derives from the force, truth and universality of the ideas which it took for its law, and from the passion with which it could inspire these ideas, a unique and still living power; it is – it will probably long remain – the greatest, the most animating event in history. And as no sincere passion for the things of the mind, even though it turn out in many respects an unfortunate passion, is ever quite thrown away and quite barren of good, France has reaped from hers one fruit – the natural and legitimate fruit, though not precisely the grand fruit she expected; she is the country in Europe where *the people* is most alive.

It is still true of our Irish rebels (and it must have been true of many rebels all over Europe at the time of the Revolution) that it was upon the emotional content of the Revolution that they seized and not on its intellectual content. The result is that the whole of Irish patriotic literature ever since has either concerned itself with matters of sentiment rather than thought; or with interim solutions of immediate problems that time has since dealt with otherwise. Irish political thought is, to this day, in its infancy.

THE PRIESTS

ALTHOUGH Christianity came to Ireland in the fifth century, the Catholic priest, without whom any picture of modern Ireland is unthinkable, does not occupy a central position in that picture until the nineteenth century. The distinction is a political one, for it has to be accepted that what gave the Catholic clergy their social prominence was their political influence, and that without that influence the priest would no more have taken the centre of the stage in Irish life than the parson in English life. When the priest did not possess this political influence he was, indeed, in his own religious realm, adored, feared and obeyed; one could nevertheless describe whole centuries without one personal reference to the robe – no matter how often one considered it necessary to keep on insisting that the people were devotedly Catholic. See, for example, the fourteenth and fifteenth centuries.

What I mean by political influence had better be defined at once. I mean, quite simply, influence in the political arena. I do not mean that the priest always exercises this influence for the mere sake of power; or that he is not fully entitled to this influence; or that he always employs this influence which he possesses; or, using the word 'priest' as a personification of the Church, that he ever exercises this influence for the mere purposes of party politics; nor, indeed, do I think that he has any interest in these matters except where they concern religion; though what concerns religion is, of course, the debatable point. An Early Closing Act is hardly likely to concern religion. The early or late closing of taverns may or may not. The closing or opening of brothels does. So does contraception, mixed marriages and divorce. In *all* of these matters the priest can exercise a powerful influence in the political arena. Until that power came his way he was not the prominent figure in Irish life that he became in the nineteenth century and still is.

Throughout the earlier centuries the priest was never a prominent figure. The prominent figures, then, were monks. That was because monasticism was the focus of early Irish Christianity, and even after the Norman Reformation changed that by establishing an episcopal organization, it is the abbot and the abbey which still attracted most attention until the Elizabethan age. Then, for the first time, the priest begins to exercise a political influence, though not so much the seculars as the orders. The 'friar' is the most adored as the Jesuit is the most admired figure of the sixteenth century. (The word 'adored' is taken from the report of Capuys, the imperial ambassador in London, writing about Ireland to Charles V in 1534, and he also uses the words 'obeyed' and 'feared'.)

These influential clerical figures were not always Irishmen. The outstanding religious figures of the sixteenth-century 'Holy War' of James Fitzmaurice were Oviedo, a Spanish Franciscan, and Dr Nicholas Sanders, an English Jesuit. The great clerical figure of the seventeenth-century Confederate Wars was the Italian Archbishop of Fermo, John Baptist Rinuccini. But the brunt of the work of the Counter-Reformation was done by Irish priests. Two of the earliest martyrs were Bishop O'Healy of Mayo, and his comrade Father O'Rourke, who landed in Dingle a short while before James Fitzmaurice and Sanders spread in the winds of Kerry the papal standard they brought with them from Rome. The most notable victim of the period was the papal Archbishop of Cashel, Dermot O'Hurley, tortured and executed in Dublin in 1584. Under James this persecution of Catholicism began to make the priest a personification of that powerful combination of political and religious resistance to English rule which was, for a time, to become basic in Irish nationalism. The recipe was established by Cromwell under whom – it should be enough, at this time, to recall but one horribly picturesque item from many cruel edicts – it became law that any man who wanted to earn £5 need but produce the head of a wolf or of a priest, it did not matter which.

The eighteenth century elevated the priest spiritually in proportion as it debased him socially. He became the only intelligent companion the people had – excepting the travelling Gaelic poets. But, both priest and poet were now weak *political* reeds. Right up to the union of Britain and Ireland in 1801, the terminus of the century, the constant policy of the Irish hierarchy was to proclaim its loyalty to the Throne in the hope of winning at least some reliefs from the Penal Laws. Thus, the Catholic bishops, like the Catholic aristocrats, were in favour of the Union of Great Britain and Ireland — being grossly deceived by Pitt into believing that Catholic Relief would follow. The coldly disapproving attitude of the clergy to rebellion, let alone disloyalty, fostered by the Gallicanism of Maynooth, persisted into the nineteenth century, long after the death of the man who finally made the priest a representative national figure — that great demagogue and organizer of Catholic resistance, Dan O'Connell.

The dates of his life-work are from about 1805 to 1845. In those forty years O'Connellism gradually undermined the conservatism of Maynooth. After all, the priests might understandably draw back from Tone's doctrines of French Republicanism and Irish armed resistance: they could hardly hold back from O'Connell's constitutional fight for Catholic Emancipation, or his later fight against Tithes. Not that they flocked at once to O'Connell's side. On the contrary, his letters give many indications of popular resentment against them for their inaction at the start of his fight, especially on the question of the Government's claim to hand pick Catholic bishops, to which the entire Board of Maynooth at one time agreed and on which some of the most influential bishops, such as the Archbishop of Dublin, constantly wobbled. ('There is a tendency already to substitute friars for any priests who are supposed to favour the Veto.' Or, again, 'You cannot conceive anything more lively than the abhorrence of the Vetoistical plans among the people at large. I really think they will go near to desert all such clergymen as do not now take an active part on the question. The Methodists were never in so fair a way of making converts.')

Gradually O'Connell rallied the mass of the priests behind him. Once in the arena they fought manfully. Before he died he was to find that he was behind them. Inevitably and properly, they had kept their autonomy, until at the close of his career, he found himself being dictated to by the bishops — on the controversial question of popular and higher education, the national schools and the University question.

By 1850, then, that terrible bogy-man of the nineteenth century all over Europe, the 'Priest in Politics', has arrived in Ireland. In other words, the priest in a country about ninety per cent Catholic is the barometer of the political emancipation of the majority. His rise followed their rise. By 1850 the Catholic Church in Ireland had a well-established seminary in Maynooth. It was not a wealthy foundation. The original grant, of 1795, was a mere £8,000, which the Government did not increase until 1807 and then, in the face of a bigoted opposition, only to something under £10,000. Why there should have been such opposition is now hard to understand since Maynooth was loyal beyond suspicion: ever since the day of its foundation it had been strictly enjoined by the Vatican to give an example of unswerving loyalty to the Crown 'at all times and places'.

A frank history of that struggling Maynooth would make moving reading: the internal tensions between Irishmen and foreigners, the insistent poverty, the naïveties and crudities of the poor peasant students who must often have worn the patience of their teachers – at least once there were student riots behind which one can feel the patriotic passions of peasant Ireland breaking through the French rigorism of the seminary. Things did ease a little in 1845 when the grant rose to £23,360, with £30,000 for buildings: but a bitter price had to be paid for this Government assistance – lack of freedom, lay visitations, discussions in Parliament, inquiries by Government commissions. One may imagine how any Oxford college would have loathed that sort of thing from its own Government, not to speak of a foreign government.

When the grant was commuted for a capital sum in 1869, at the time of Church Disestablishment, these inspections and controls were removed and Maynooth could straighten its back, although now poorer by half. The bishops had £369,000 on hand, buildings and lands, somewhere around £15,000 for annual burses, and students' fees: the whole of which, invested, would not bring in half of the former grant. (The Disestablished Church was, at the same date, receiving about eight million pounds in capital values.) The priest was now completely

free, and established in his freedom. Persecution was gone for
ever; his was a recognized profession; he had an enormous
local personal influence; his flock had the franchise and they
were the majority of the population. This man, who had once
been hunted like a wild beast, then barely tolerated, then grudg-
ingly acknowledged as a citizen, was now a power that no local
or national politician could ignore.

From very soon after emancipation the priest begins to enter contemporary fiction – in Carleton, Lever, Lover and others
– and one may see him in general outline as he struck observers,
prejudiced and otherwise. He rarely comes from the middle
classes, he is farmer-stock, often put through college at a great
sacrifice by poor parents; he is not very cultivated, he has not
been cut off from the people by his education, they feel him as
one of themselves. (In passing, at least some contemporary
politicians felt that when Peel proposed a University for the
Catholics and increased the Maynooth grant he had in mind in
the hope of attracting priests from a higher class, and of cultiva-
ting them away from the peasantry.) All these novelists agree
on the priest's great influence in local politics: their charac-
terizations imply various explanations for it.

One of the earliest novels dealing with priests sympathetically is Banim's *Father Connell* (1840). I find it sentimental.
Others have approved of it wholeheartedly. 'The character is
one of the noblest in fiction. He is the ideal Irish priest, almost
childlike in simplicity, pious, lavishly charitable, meek and long-
suffering but terrible when circumstances roused him to action.'*
There the priest's influence is moral. At the other end of the
scale is *Misther O'Ryan* by Edward M'Nulty (1894) in which
the priest is an ugly, whiskey-drinking, vulgar fellow. His influence is that of a bully and a political intriguer. In both of
these books one may confidently perceive not objectively observed human beings but personifications of the same political
sympathies and prejudices that one sometimes finds in Balzac's
novels.

Most writers, if they do not follow those extreme lines, see
the priest in one of three aspects – the jovial, hunting, hearty

A Reader's Guide to Irish Fiction, Rev. Stephen Brown, S. J., Dublin,
1919.

priest, who is really a 'good fellow' in clerical garb; or the rigorous, unbending, saintly and generally rather inhuman ascetic – the patriarch of his flock; or the man whose life is one long psychological problem. In one or other of these aspects he has been drawn over and over again during the last century, by Lever, Banim, Carleton, Griffin, George Moore, Shaw (see the contrasts of two types in *John Bull's Other Island*), Liam O'Flaherty, Paul Vincent Carroll and others. Only two novelists have had inner access, Gerald O'Donovan, who was a lapsed priest – he was a Modernist, or an ecumenist before his time – and Canon Sheehan; though in their novels one feels the defect inherent in a professional exclusiveness – the enclosed reference, the *a priori* assumptions. Sheehan can only draw priests, and only as priests, and poor minor characters – these are the best of all his characters, such as a chapel-woman (half-char, half-sacristan) or a beggar, or some bedridden old saint whom he must have often visited and dearly loved. O'Donovan's animus is a wider professional dissatisfaction with the Church.

The key to the nature of the priest is that he is elusively twofold. His secret is that of all the arcane professions. It is impossible to isolate, in any one of his acts, his personal from his professional elements. What the military academy does to the cadet, what the law schools do to the law student, the seminary does to the young cleric. Each one makes a sacrifice of his personal liberty, of the single-mindedness, or unity of his personality, in order to achieve the enlargement of power that comes with membership of a great professional caste. (Balzac recognizes this in his *Curé de Campagne*, the better, I think, of the only two successful novels written about priesthood: the other, Fogazzaro's *Il Santo*. Some might add part of *Le Rouge et le Noir*.) Because of this sacrifice one can never see the priest exclusively as a priest: his human personality is dedicated but not suppressed. But neither can we see him exclusively as a man: he has risen superior to normal human values, intercourse and sympathies. And he is cut off from the lay world by celibacy.

If all this puts the priest in a doubtless sometimes troubling relationship to himself it puts him in a powerfully strategic relationship to the public. One can see this over and over in the puzzlement, sometimes the exasperation, of the layman at a loss to know where the human element ends and the professional element begins. The priest, like the soldier, will always explain his public acts in professional terms, never in merely human terms; and although the angry layman – like Daniel O'Connell on more occasions than one – may privately sniff at clerical 'opportunism' he must hold his peace: because it may be so, and, in any case, the artillery of argument against him is colossal, not to mention the deadly power of the snipers and the discomfort of such fragmentation bombs as the cry of 'anti-clerical', 'anti-God', 'Red', 'Leftist', 'lay-bishop', and that most devastating bomb of all, on which is chalked – 'Yah! Intellectual!'*

Let us state the fundamentals. The priest is fighting an immortal fight with mortal weapons. It is all very well for Lecky to say that the rise of liberalism has declared the union of politics and theology an anachronism by pronouncing their divorce. The priest does not recognize divorce. For him the two worlds are inseparable; the kingdom of earth is but a battleground for the kingdom of heaven, and he will advance and retreat on that ground just like a soldier. No Irish priest, for example, objects to lay control of education on principle – there is no

---

*Here I use the words 'priest' and 'church' in a local sense; but the Church as a whole, or as we say 'the Vatican', is the model for the Church in Ireland. See on this a very interesting essay: 'The Diplomacy of the Vatican', by Daniel Binchy in *International Affairs*, January 1946, reprinted in *The Bell*, May 1946:

The Vatican as a religious Power and the Vatican as a political Power cannot really be separated, but for a great many purposes they have to be distinguished. . . . The relation between politics and morality is an extremely difficult problem, and I do not believe that the Papacy, any more than any other Power, has succeeded in solving it. One result of this is that papal pronouncements on questions of international morality have to be made with an eye to the repercussions of such statements on the interest of the Church, not merely in the world as a whole but in one particular area; hence the tendency so often noted in such pronouncements, to enunciate only the most general principles. Again the necessity of considering the interests of the Catholic Church as a whole in a changing society leads to what may be called flexibility – or, if you prefer, opportunism – in various aspects of papal policy. More important still the wider view which is generally taken in the Curia often comes into conflict with local nationalism.

such theological principle. Indeed, when he thinks about the laity all he ever considers is the quality of its thought in the political temper of its times. Maynooth accepted a large measure of lay control in 1795 through those constant inspections and visitations; and from a foreign government at that. In 1799 the entire board of bishops at Maynooth agreed to subject *all* Catholic bishops to the *visa* of that foreign government, which is surely the apex of lay control? From its foundation it promised unswerving loyalty to that inspecting government and installed professors guaranteed to maintain fanatically that this loyalty was dogmatic. Nevertheless the Church does not want lay control of education – simply because it does not trust its own flock to put immortal ends before mortal.

In short, the Catholic Church does not – within the broadest limits of human justice, and indeed often tolerating human and even clerical persecution to a degree astonishing to the layman – care a rap about any human or political matter. It watches and waits and bargains all the time, *solely in its own interests as a Church*. It is a human institution guided by Heaven – wise in a human way. It does not engage personally in the human struggle. But wherever power emerges it will follow after – to bargain with it. It is, as a Church, superior to all merely human sympathies, however it may severally be agonized by the chaos of life and affairs about it. It will condemn the patriot today and do its heavenly business with him tomorrow – if he wins: but if the patriot counts on his support until he does win he is unreasonable if only because he would himself be the first to resent the interference of the Church on some other occasion. It is thus no exaggeration to say that the patriot, fighting for his country, hoping for success, must, if a loyal son of the Church, gamble his soul on a purely human victory. His dilemma contains an immortal irony. It rarely amuses those involved.

There can be no arguing about this. The law of obedience is binding. The layman must abide by the rules or, like Ivan Karamazov, 'hand back the ticket'. In 1922, for example, when a Civil War was raging in Ireland between the 'Republican' forces of Mr de Valera and the 'National' forces of the Free State Government the Ordinary of the Diocese of Cork issued a

Pastoral warning to his flock that: 'According to the declaration of the bishops of Ireland the killing of National soldiers is murder'; and that priests were doing their duty in refusing the sacraments to those who disobeyed. Any Catholic who disobeyed – and they numbered thousands – sinned. Again, the Ordinary of a diocese may, so to speak, 'invent' a mortal sin by laying down a new rule at any moment. For many years past the Ordinary of the Archdiocese of Dublin declared it a mortal sin for Catholics deliberately to send their children, without his express permission, to Dublin University (non-Catholic), leaving only four alternatives open to the devout: to obey without question as most did; to obey and appeal to Rome – a tedious and unpromising process which nobody tried; to evade, for example by sending their children to Oxford or Cambridge, as a few did, or by transferring their residence outside the border of the Archdiocese to a diocese where the Ordinary had not made the same rule. The priest does not, however, often press the laity so hard. He prefers persuasions, he bides his time, he is infinitely patient. He allows the fullest interpretation to Burke's, 'It is no inconsiderable part of wisdom to know how much of an evil ought to be tolerated'.

This University question is informative. It first appeared in the 1840s so that it is an old question now, though it was then, for Ireland, a rather late introduction to a problem that had long troubled other countries in Europe – the accommodation of Church and State in education.

It falls into two stages. The operative date for the first stage is 1849. With the ending of the Penal Laws and the arrival of Catholic emancipation the British Government wished to found a University in Ireland for the mass of the people. Peel proposed and founded in 1849 what came to be known as Queen's Colleges. They were non-denominational, under secular control, and no provision was made for teaching philosophy or history according to Catholic viewpoints. The younger idealists and rebels (the Young Irelanders) would have welcomed any scheme which would provide higher education for the people; the bishops and O'Connell rejected it; and when the scheme developed in spite of them, the bishops laboured to keep the middle classes from sending their children to these Queen's

Colleges. We cannot here discuss this complex and controversial question in detail. We can only consider the one point before us. On that head, it is evident that the refusal of the bishops to tolerate the Queen's Colleges was – whether wise or not – a perfectly legitimate and proper refusal. They had been condemned on all sides, by Catholic laymen in Ireland, by the Catholic bishops, by Conservative members of the House of Commons. All that this stage of the question offers, therefore, is a good illustration of the normal and legitimate influence of the priest in the political arena.

The operative date for the second stage is 1852 when Cardinal Paul Cullen persuaded John Henry Newman to come to Dublin and found a Catholic University in opposition to Peel's 'godless colleges'. Newman had a very sad time of it with the Irish bishops, and he soon found himself at loggerheads even with Cardinal Cullen – over the amount of control, if any, which the laity might be permitted in the Catholic University. He saw that Cullen was utterly suspicious of the rebelly spirit then alive in Irish political thought, what His Grace called 'Young Irelandism'. 'Dr Cullen', Newman wrote to a friend, 'seems to think that Young Irelandism is the natural product of the lay mind everywhere, if let to grow freely': and as a corollary – once more distrusting his own flock – would not tolerate *any* measure of lay control. To this Newman could never agree: he said that if Dr Cullen's views were to prevail the University would 'simply be priest-ridden. . . . I mean men who do not know literature and science will have the direction of the teaching. I cannot conceive the professors taking part in this. They will be simply scrubs'.

Newman speaking again:

On both sides of the Channel the deep difficulty is the jealousy and fear which is entertained in high quarters of the laity. . . . Nothing great or living can be done except when men are self-governed and independent.

This antipathy to the laity certainly was, to some extent, Anglade* and Delahogue and MacHale and 'J.K.L.' all over again: a political French-born terror of the 'Red Spectre', as

*Vide, p. 94 ff.

the official biographer of Maynooth College has called it. It was not just Dr Cullen's personal experiences in Rome that lay behind this episcopal distrust of the layman and the rebel – he had seen the Republican Mazzini take possession of Vatican property, and had personally saved the College of Propaganda by persuading the American Minister to float the Stars and Stripes over it. Dr MacHale was just as adamant. '*There should not longer be any doubt or ambiguity regarding the exclusive right of the bishops to legislate and to make all appointments.*' (*Letters*, 20 February 1852.) In the century before, that devoted Catholic John Keogh, with Tone, had developed a scheme for a Catholic Seminary, and had been met, to Keogh's fury (and he was the mildest of men), by precisely the same maddening refusal to trust the laity.

Keogh could not understand this. He thought it unreasonable. And humanly speaking it was unreasonable. But there the churchman slips away from us; for what has 'humanly speaking' to do with him? The bishops distrusted the Keogh-Tone collaboration, and from their point of view, considering Tone's French sympathies, very naturally so. In short it is obvious that although Dr Cullen had a political antipathy to the Young Irelanders, as Dr Egan had to the United Irishmen, nobody will ever pin down Dr Cullen's distrust of his people to a purely secular-political – not to speak of anti-nationalist – bias.

After all, when Newman returned to England he met precisely the same distrust of the laity in Cardinal Manning. Liberalism was in the air. Even Newman feared that Mill and Darwin and Huxley were undermining traditional belief. So might Manning, but he relied on the lymph of authority. Newman was an intellectual; his whole turn of mind was speculative and analytical; he foresaw, years before ecumenism, that not authority but knowledge, not an absolutist church but a teaching church working hand in hand with an educated and independent-minded laity, was the only possible answer to the agnostic danger. It is a matter of record that when he raised such questions the priests, whether of England or Ireland, mopped and mowed and clutched their crucifixes as if he were introducing Beelzebub in person to a gullible and incompetent laity.

(This is, also, the usual contempt of the professional for the layman.)

The laity welcomed Newman's fighting attitude. New ideas were pouring in on them in the streets and the clubs and the universities and men like W. G. Ward and the future Lord Acton simply had to have access to the replies. Newman had said, 'Great changes before now have taken place in the Church's course and new aspects of her aboriginal doctrines have suddenly come forth,' and the laymen wanted to know what those new aspects were and what light they threw on modern scientific and biblical research. But the story of this long struggle between this inquiring mind of a harassed laity and the traditionally suspicious church has been told several times, including the melancholy climax when Newman was denounced in Rome and delated to the Holy See, as the agent of Catholic Liberalism in England! If time has since proved Newman right and Manning wrong, and if poor Newman meantime suffered agonies of mind and soul, well, that is but the story of the patriot all over again; and many and many a patriot has had to be just as agile as Newman, in a different field, to evade destruction.

In Ireland the struggle was not on an intellectual plane. There, politics entered into it much more, because the struggle circled around much more primitive and passionate questions – such as, 'When is it lawful for a suppressed nation to rebel?', a question to which, of course, there is no answer. Fenianism was rife in Ireland in the 1860s – the latest successors to the Young Irelanders and the United Irishmen. An entry in O'Neill Daunt's *Diary* puts their dilemma succinctly:

September 12th, 1865: When the priests condemned Fenianism in the confessional and refused the sacraments to persons connected with it many of the Fenian youths of Cork gave up going to confession to priests who had been educated at Maynooth; but some of them confessed to priests brought up in foreign seminaries.

But would he not be a very shallow observer who would attempt to say that this condemnation was either purely political, or purely theological? One cannot, I repeat, isolate the elements. The priest is indissolubly of heaven and earth: which is what makes him so slow to commit himself in any earthly fight, and — I say it quite objectively and without a trace of irony, for he is, from his point of view, quite right — it is this also that makes him come out from his cautious seclusion only when he finds the flood in full spate around him. The priest was slow to support O'Connell. He was slow to support the Home Rule movement. (Another entry of O'Neill Daunt's *Diary*, September 1870, speaks of a letter from T. D. Sullivan complaining about 'the small number of priests who have heretofore joined the Home Rule Movement'.) He was also slow to support the Sinn Fein movement. And so, likewise, he is, generally, slow also to condemn. It is the layman in politics who forces the priest into politics, or, if one prefers, urges him before him — always *at his peril*. Conversely is it not the layman who complains when the priest enters politics without him?

A small, but telling, illustration of the Church's indifference to 'the Nation' as such is offered by the Irish Language Revival. Enthusiasts sometimes complain that the Church in Ireland is not behind the Revival Movement. Why should it be? And if, historically, the priest has been rather opposed to the Language Movement than otherwise, why should he not be? All one's sympathies, mine do at any rate, will go out to that courageous man Dr O'Hickey, Professor of Gaelic at Maynooth, who was sacked by Maynooth in 1909 because he fought openly for the introduction of compulsory Irish into the National University, who tried to fight his case to Rome, and who, like many another, died without receiving any decision. If the Catholic Church in Ireland then regarded the Language Revival as unlikely to be of assistance to it, it was fully entitled to withhold its official support. The Language enthusiast, like every other enthusiast, may rest assured that the Church in Ireland will, like Lord Chesterfield to Dr Johnson, throw him a rope only when he is on dry land. And if the somewhat dampened enthusiast could imagine himself transmogrified into a board of bishops he will agree that he, in their place, would do just the same, or else his imagination has not worked hard enough.

The modern Irish politician has, I think, begun to understand all this. And I should not be surprised if the Church in Ireland is also beginning to see the position clearly. There have been some burnings of fingers on both sides, and there is an old inheritance of distrust. (The Government, as late as 1968, included men who in 1922, as Republicans in arms, defied the episcopal warning that the killing of National soldiers was murder; and they won their way to power in 1932 in the teeth of some strong clerical opposition.) In 1946, when the primary teachers went on strike, the Archbishop of Dublin made it evident that his sympathies were with them: the Government absolutely refused to accept His Grace as intermediary. When a Bishop Dignan produced a scheme for a comprehensive system of Social Insurance in 1945 the Minister for Local Government repulsed it acidly. A weighty Report from a Commission on Vocational Representation, which had been sitting for years under the chairmanship of the Bishop of Galway, was the occasion of some further sharp exchanges with another Minister; and the Report has since been silently interred. What do these three incidents mean? Do they mean that the priest, now that we have our own government, is only too willing to take a hand in purely secular political and social questions? Hardly. Education has always been a rope pulled from two ends. Vocational representation would involve large political changes that might affect the influence of the Church. That leaves us with just one example not directly of clerical interest, social insurance. In that case the priest was refreshingly more advanced and humane than the politician who rebuffed him. These rebuffs may suggest, on the other hand, that the State is becoming jealous of its autonomy.

Who would lose out if the autonomy of the State were threatened by the Church? Indubitably, the Church: for the following reasons. In Ireland the Church holds her power by the old medieval bond of Faith. She does not need political techniques, as the Church in other more secularized countries does; and if she does not need them, she must be held unjustified in using them. The Catholic Church in Ireland is *immune*, to borrow a word from Lord Acton — 'The Pope is at the head of a great *immunitas*, like many other prelates'. Immune she should remain. But it was Acton, again, who insisted with satisfaction that in all secular States the existence of great classes, nobles, *clergy*, etc., limits the State power; and he deplored the fact that at the date in which he was writing (January 1862) the 'great class of clergy is the mere instrument of the sovereign'. 'Liberty,' he concluded, 'consists *in radice* in the preservation of an inner sphere exempt from State power'. A Church, overtly or tacitly, deliberately or unwittingly, in alliance or in conjunction with the State, must sooner or later threaten not so much the liberty of the State as its own liberty, become identified in the public mind with the State, cease to be an 'inner sphere', and leave itself wide open to purely political criticism. It need not be added that the quality of the liberty which will exist inside any 'inner sphere' will, of course, depend on how civilized and humanized that envelope, that sanctuary itself is. This is the great test of the Catholic Church in Ireland today.

In Ireland, today, priests and laity still rest at ease – with one qualification. Only one group is held at arm's length, the writers or intellectuals. They, at a far, far remove from that unapproachably great man whose name we have invoked several times, Newman, see that the intellectual struggle is upon Ireland's doorstep. They, like all Catholic intellectuals the world over, want questions to be raised, and answered. The Church still relies obstinately on the weapon of rigid authority. It could safely do this as long as it was concerned with an Ireland protected and sheltered from the world. This isolation is now a dream. Walls of censorship were erected to keep out books and films that raise awkward questions. Practically every Irish writer of note was at one time or another thrown to the lambs, i.e., in the interests of the most unsophisticated banned in his own country, some over and over again. But the air was uncensorable. Vulgarity and cheapness could not be censored. Films are still censored but only for blatantly objectionable things. Their essential triviality, their debasing cheapness of thought, their tinsel dreams infect the most remote villages. Above all a constant flow and reflow of emigrants flood in the world outside with all its questions, challenges and bright temptations. In so far as the priest has long seemed content he has seemed to the Irish writer to be either excessively cautious or excessively lazy, or to be making exactly the same mistake that Cardinal Manning made in England in the sixties.

One may, for instance, be appalled to think that there is not in Ireland today a single layman's Catholic periodical to which one could apply the adjective 'inquiring', or even 'intelligent', in the sense in which it could have been applied to Newman's *Rambler*; and that with the exception of one professional organ and one admirable Jesuit quarterly, the clerical papers are all trivial – a state of affairs that might almost justify the Irish intellectual in echoing Newman's famous phrase about the 'temporary suspense of the *Ecclesia Docens*'. There is no *The Month*, no *Blackfriars*, no *Dublin Review*, no *Commonweal*, no periodical remotely like Emmanual Mounier's *Esprit*. The tragedy of all this is, of course, that the priest and the writer ought to be fighting side by side, if for nothing else than the rebuttal of the vulgarity that is pouring daily into the vacuum left in the popular mind by the dying out of the old traditional life. But there can be no such common ground as long as the Church follows the easy way of authority instead of discussion or takes the easy way out by applying to all intellectual ideas the test of their effect on the poor and the ignorant.

Looking at the Catholic Church in Ireland in relation to the modern ecumenical movement one has to record that it was among the slowest-moving members of the universal Catholic Church. The historical reason for this has been touched on several times in the preceding pages. The Church in Ireland is a victim of one of the most influential facts in our history, namely that the Reformation in England coincided with the Conquest in Ireland. The result is that when we lost our native aristocracy after the Williamite wars (1691), but still held firmly to our traditional faith, we were left with a purely popular or peasant church, much too poor and too harassed to develop an intellectual life either among its priests or its people. In the circumstances the Church, not unnaturally, found it easier to rule by command rather than by advice or persuasion. It is still locked in that imperious tradition, unable or unwilling to admit that its flock has been developing ahead of it.

Some of the resultant tensions have already been mentioned. One modern instance is specially worthy of mention. In 1968 a Commission set up by the government to inquire into the Constitution of the Irish state suggested that in the interest of Irish political unity, and of justice to Irish minorities divorce should henceforth be given legal recognition. At once the Catholic Primate issued a protest, not so much stressing the principle as the practice: meaning, in effect, that he feared that even Catholics might be tempted to avail of legalized divorce. In practice, of course, no Catholic could do so, otherwise than by ceasing to be a Catholic. This His Eminence obviously wished to prevent, not, however, by advice and persuasion alone but by the old, traditional method of rule by command, to be further enforced by the secular law.

It is worth remembering that in this matter the practice of other European countries which may be called Catholic varies. In France divorce is legal, and not merely is civil marriage legal, but it alone is legal – any couple who marry solely in church are considered by French law to be living in concubinage, their children legally bastards. Loyal Catholics in France are not disturbed by this: they simply do not avail of divorce, and quietly supplement their church marriage by a civil ceremony, or vice versa. In Italy, Mussolini made divorce illegal and, as for marriage, adopted the common compromise of insisting that every church marriage must be registered with the state before it can be considered legal. He outlawed divorce for two reasons. Firstly because, although he had no religious convictions of any kind about anything, he saw, with his usual penetrating understanding of the Italian mind, that the mass of his people did not want divorce, being, as they are, utterly devoted to that nerve-centre of their lives, the family nexus. Secondly, he wanted as many Italian children as possible to grow up under Fascism as cannon-fodder for his future imperial wars. If any useful conclusion may be drawn for those two Catholic countries it is that while Mussolini was clever and corrupting – after all, thousands of Italians, thanks to him, are now living in concubinage, and contracepting to avoid producing legal bastards – Napoleon was more humane and more just in recognizing legal divorce for those who wanted it without recommending it to anybody who did not.

One might further conclude that Irish Catholics – and indeed Irish people of every Christian denomination – might be trusted to act as their French counterparts do. However, the old habit of Rule by Command is so deeply rooted here that it is likely to persist for a long time to come. On the other hand the younger generation strongly resents it, is far more outspoken in its resentment than it ever was before, and – as has been happening for many generations in Italy – is likely soon to reduce the word Catholic (as distinct from 'practising Catholic') to a merely nominal value unless their Church learns quickly that these younger people, probably the best part of modern Irish life, are the scattered beginnings of an intellectual élite that with skill it could still hitch to its star.

That an Irish government should, even if only through a Commission, raise the idea of legal divorce is, then, a healthy sign of the times. Nevertheless, it is revealing also in a disturbing way: there was no widespread public discussion of the matter, and what little discussion there was in occasional letters to the press, was emotional rather than intelligent. On the one side somebody would say – as if this ended the matter – that Christ held that whom God hath joined no man may put asunder; or appeal with passion to something called 'the national tradition'. On the other side an appeal would be made on behalf of minority rights. The matter is further obfuscated by the fact that the Protestant tradition, especially in the north-east, is even more conservative and less intelligent than the Catholic tradition in the south. Nobody ever discusses divorce *per se*. Nobody, for example, asks how do we know that God joined any pair in marriage; or what 'join' means; or whether God is mocked by being assumed to be responsible for human mistakes; or whether Christ in uttering that famous sentence was not speaking in the totally different context of unjust wife-desertion by the Jews of the time. But, as I have already pointed out, where could such intelligent discussions take place? We have not got the independent periodicals for it, and our Radio and Television – though there have been some refreshingly frank, if all too brief spurts of liberal opinion on both – are inobtrusively and indirectly, but none the less firmly controlled with quiet caution by the State.

12

THE WRITERS

THREE creative events – the only kind of events that we are concerned with here – occurred in nineteenth-century Ireland. They were Catholic emancipation, land reform, and the literary revival. The first gave the vote to the masses and began modern parliamentary politics, conducted, up to 1922, in the British House of Commons. From it came a series of Land Acts, which, bit by bit, changed a dependent tenantry into an independent yeomanry, a process now almost completed. In the literary revival we get the summary of the whole of this transformation of an ancient race, first defeated, then depressed, then virtually stripped of its traditions, into a modern – or a more or less modern – people, for the process continues, and is far from complete. The new literature did more than summarize, it was itself an active agent. It was more, far more, than a number of isolated writers 'expressing themselves'. It was a whole people giving tongue, and by that self-articulation approaching nearer than ever before to intellectual and imaginative freedom.

Irish literature in Gaelic, like the Irish aristocracy, had received in the seventeenth century blows from which it never recovered. Being the literature of a caste it died with the caste. What of it persisted into the eighteenth century, and in a ragtag-and-bobtail way into the nineteenth century, was the kind of survival which, by its very persistence, achieves honour mingled with pity, alike for what was patently lost along the way and for what more is certain to be lost in the future.

A literature, one feels, must justify itself on its literary merits, not on factitious appeal. An exclusively patriotic or nostalgic interest in literature makes it of merely sentimental interest, relegates it to the bottom drawer with baby's shoes and mother's wedding-veil. 'Look,' one says, with tears welling, 'this was written by one of our poor, down-trodden people in dark and evil days. We must always preserve it.' By all means, let us preserve everything, even the humblest and crudest implement of man. Do not let us then give it a value greater than its intrinsic value. Some of the Gaelic poetry written in the eighteenth century, by the last surviving members of the caste, has genuine merit; most of it has little merit; what has a real merit, and has proved it by its living, developing persistence – which is not a museum persistence – is the lore of the common people. This is vital. It has now gone underground. It is, so to speak, being forgotten consciously. It nevertheless beats like a great earth-throb in the subconsciousness of the race. The Irish language is thus become the runic language of modern Ireland. Even though only a dwindling few think overtly in it all of us can, through it, touch, however dimly, a buried part of ourselves of which we are normally unaware. Through Gaelic we remember ancestrally – are again made very old and very young. As compared with the literary survivals in Gaelic of the last two hundred years, the popular, vocal lore or folklore is in this way infinitely richer, more imaginative and more inspiring. This, however, depends strictly on the number of people, mostly along the western seaboard now – probably less than 30,000 – who use Gaelic as their natural speech, as the language of bed and board, and only through whom, and only with whom, one can live back into the old life-ways.

As for Gaelic learned for patriotic reasons, spoken only very occasionally by townsmen, it is a literary key only to the comparatively poor storehouses of the eighteenth- and nineteenth-century poets. It does not open the doors to the really rich past of the old Gaelic world, back through the middle ages to the times of the sagas. To open those doors one has to master Old and Middle Irish, a task which demands many years of hard and patient study.

The inspiration of the men who first set the modern literary revival on its way was a purely patriotic one. These men were the rebelly group known as the Young Irelanders, whose rise we may date at the year 1845, by the first issue of their paper *The Nation*. They thus came after Catholic emancipation, were contemporaneous with O'Connell, took part in the Tithe War, the fight for the repeal of the Union of Britain and Ireland, the arguments over education, the start of the land troubles, and welled over, through their successors, into the parliamentary fight in Westminster. They found a depressed and uneducated peasantry, saw the first great waves of emigration to America, watched the dying-out of the native language. To them O'Connell, who, as a pragmatic politician, had no time for Gaelic and said that he saw it die without regret, was too much of a materialist to build up the soul of the people.

To them, lost in their own high idealism, appeals on the score of Ireland's material poverty were almost base; they thought of glory, not of finance, and they ransacked the past that O'Connell had kicked aside. They tried to learn from little books the language O'Connell spoke as a child, and thereafter only when addressing the peasants of the western seaboards. They would meet on the roads old men who were to O'Connell so many votes and little else, and because of the memories these old men preserved they saw, behind their apparent illiteracy, superficial roughness or even boorishness, something like the last rays of their sun-god. How angry they would have been to hear O'Connell called King of the Beggars - not because they could deny his kingship but because they felt themselves as the descendants of kings. These – Mangan, Davis, Gavan Duffy, Meagher, Mitchel, Doheny, and others – created in verse and prose, for they were able men of letters, image after image of the legendary greatness of their people, and they appealed to the country in the name of its former glory.*

All that I have already said about the way in which the Rebel spends and wastes himself is true a hundredfold of these men. They did not devote their great talents to literature for its own sake: they devoted them to literature in the interests of politics. Their interest was in functional literature. Their literary work suffered accordingly; their political influence prospered.

Before a literary movement could develop in a strictly literary way Irish writers had to purify literature of this political impurity. The first historian of that later period went so far, and rightly, as to define the process as one of Dedavisization – Thomas Davis being the outstanding creator of this politico-literary journalism of the 1840s. Yet, in one most vital way the Young Irelanders were wise in their generation: they insisted on the use of native material. To show the absolute rightness

*From *King of the Beggars*, O'Faolin. (London, 1938.)

of this let us look, very shortly, at the good (and bad) example of one of their predecessors, the Cork poet Jeremiah Joseph Callanan, who died in 1829.

This poet is remembered today for ballads and songs that propose him as the first really popular Irish poet writing in English: see his fine poem on 'Gougane Barra', his ballad 'The Revenge of Donal Cawm', his translation of some of the really good Gaelic songs of the eighteenth century, such as 'O say my brown Drimin, thou silk of the kine', or 'The Convict of Clonmel'. Yet, the truth is that in so far as he was a popular poet he was popular in spite of himself, almost by accident, and his story is a revelation of how easily a poet may miss his true inspiration. At Trinity College he won his first recognition for a poem on, of all things, 'Alexander's Restoration of the Spoils of Athens'. He wrote a sycophantic poem in praise of George IV. For years his models were English models. He called Byron the 'bard of my boyhood's love'; his 'eagle of song', his 'fountain of beauty'. The effect on a young provincial Irishman was disastrous: as one may see at one glance:

> The night was still, the air was balm,
> Soft dews around were weeping . . .

All that came of it, that is, were pleasant, pseudo-Byronic verses of which one may say that none of them go very far except in the sense that they all go much too far – from home, from life, from reality:

> Thy name to this bosom
>   Now sounds like a knell;
> My fond one, my dear one,
>   For ever farewell.

A Byron could write light songs on that theme and make them ring with passionate tenderness; not an unsophisticated Irish country lad pretending to be a Byron.

Callanan's most ambitious poem, and the poem in which he took most pride, was 'The Recluse of Inchidony'. The difference between something that is just a pose, and something that is experienced may be seen in the comparison of eight lines of 'Inchidony' with eight lines of 'Childe Harold'. Here is Callanan:

'Tis a delightful calm. There is no sound
Save the low murmur of the distant rill.
A voice from heaven is breathing all around
Bidding the earth and restless man be still.
Soft sleeps the moon on Inchidony's hill
And on the shore the shining ripples break
Gently and whisperingly at Nature's will,
Like some fair child that on its mother's cheek
Sinks fondly to repose in kisses pure and meek.

Passing over the tired clichés, is there one speck of actual observation in all that? Byron, eye fixed on the object or on the
memory does rather better:

It is the hush of the night and all between
Thy margin and the mountains dusk yet clear,
Mellowed and mingling, yet distinctly seen
Saved darkened Jura, whose capped heights appear
Precipitously steep. And drawing near.
There breathes a living fragrance from the shore
Of flowers yet fresh with childhood. On the ear
Drops the light drip of the suspended oar
Or chirps the grasshoppers one good-night carol more.

'The light drip of the suspended oar' is alone enough to make
the distinction. Callanan has not learned to revere the simple
detail of life about him, that precise stuff of which all later
Irish writers were to make their best work. He therein reflects
the lack of pride of his century. He is, in fact, the counterpart
in English of the irrealism of a great deal of eighteenth-century
Gaelic verse, forever looking sadly backwards, equally eager to
escape reality.

The Romantic movement – of which, to make another essential point, all Irish rebellion (Tone and the Young Irelanders
and the rest) is a reflection, and all Irish literature the offspring
– let Callanan out of his dilemma. Scott had resurrected the
clansman. It was part of the tradition to unearth old ballads.
Bishop Percy's *Reliques of Ancient Poetry* had appeared in
1765. Joseph Ritson had been collecting old English songs since
1783. Edward Bunting in Ireland had been collecting Irish folk-
music since 1792. Charlotte Brooke brought out her *Ancient
Irish Poetry* in 1789. Joseph Walker's *Historical Memoirs of*

the Irish Bards came in 1786. What to these collectors was antiquity was to Callanan everyday life. He seems to have suddenly looked about him, taken notice of Gaelic songs that he had often heard but never heeded, and begun to translate them. Yet, even then, he wrote patronizingly of them, not fully recognizing the gifts of the gods even as he imbibed them, calling them 'the popular songs of the lower orders', and saying, 'I present them to the public more as literary curiosities than on any other account'.

It may, at first glance, seem curious that any writer could be so purblind. It happens to writers all the time. George Moore had to exchange County Mayo for Paris to be introduced to the life of 'the lower orders' through Zola and realism. Yet, after he thus made their acquaintance in literature he did not at first write about the poor of Ireland but of England, whom he did not know at all. It was not – as he so amusingly and revealingly describes in the first volume of *Hail and Farewell* – until he met Yeats in London and heard him enthusing about the future of Irish literature that it occurred to him that there were fit and interesting subjects for his pen waiting for him back in County Mayo. One result was that excellent realistic novel about shabby-genteel landlordism in the West of Ireland, *Drama in Muslin*. We all know the similar story of how John Millington Synge was writing pieces in the Gallic mode in Paris until Yeats again stepped in and advised him to go back to Ireland and the Aran Islands. Result: *The Playboy of the Western World*. Quite a number of modern Irish writers were influenced in this illuminating way by reading such nineteenth-century Russians as Chekhov, Gogol, Dostoyevsky, Gorky, and Turgenev in whose mirrors they saw reflections of the rural life of Ireland, and how, technically, it could be depicted by any clear-eyed Irish artist. The truth seems to be that it is difficult for anyone to see anything with eyes unclouded by habit, prejudice and convention.

This curious condition of visual obliquity can become chronic among people who have been too long subject to prolonged colonial rule. I venture to give a small personal illustration. The mere names of the streets in my native city of Cork affected my mental eyesight for years as a boy. Every day I walked along a road named in honour of the Irish born Duke of Wellington.

This habitual association had a double effect on me. I took so much pride in him as an Irishman that I accepted it as a simple fact of history that the defeat of the Empire at Waterloo must be regarded as an unqualified blessing to civilization. Every other day, on my way to the Cork Free Library – to borrow another of those splendid boys' books by G. A. Henty about the glory of the British Empire – I passed a street named Anglesey Street after, I presumed, another Irishman who, I was told, lost a leg at Waterloo and gained the title of Marquis. With what awe I heard further that the current Marquis was chamberlain to Queen Mary, had been through Eton and Sandhurst, and bore such resounding honours as the Order of the Nile, the Grand Cross and Star of Afghanistan and many more such. (I may add that it was a great shock to me to discover later that the fellow was not an Irishman at all; he was not even an Englishman; he was merely a blooming Welshman.) All about me were other mesmeric memorials. Albert Quay. George's Street. Nelson Place. Union Quay. (The Union of Ireland with Britain.) Victoria Road. . . . I was particularly fascinated by a grubby street called Coburg Street when I discovered that it had been so named after one Albert Charles Francis Augustus Emmanuel, the second son of the Duke of Saxe-Coburg Gotha, who had married his cousin, Queen Victoria, at the suggestion of King Leopold I of Belgium, but contrary to the wishes of her uncle King William IV of England, the son of King George II and of Charlotte Sophia, the Princess of Mecklenburg Strelitz. And so on. It is true that many other streets were named after native Irishmen, but, educated as I was in the British colonial mode I knew nothing about them. Small wonder that a film of ignorance about Ireland covered my eyes just as effectively as it did the eyes of Jeremiah Joseph Callanan when he made his entry into Irish literature with a poem about 'Alexander's restoration of the spoils of Athens'. And small blame to him! After all, Yeats made his entry into Irish literature with a melodrama set in Morocco.

I have recounted in my autobiography how an Abbey Theatre play lifted the cataract from my eyes at the age of fifteen. Before that I had seen nothing but plays brought to Cork 'straight from the West End'. (They never needed to add the words 'of

London': where else could it be?) This play, *Patriots* by Len-
nox Robinson, is not a great play; but to me it was a revealing
and exciting experience, because it dealt not with adultery in
St John's Wood or Abbot's-Bedsock-Under-the-Hill, or with
Gordon in Khartoum, or Sir Percy Blakeney playing rings
around the revolutionary thugs of Paris under the Directorate,
but with ordinary Irish peasants, small-town shopkeepers and
farming folk any of whom could have been one of my uncles or
aunts whom I had met during my summer holidays down in
the country. The sight of them on the stage brought me strange
and wonderful news – that the streets of my native Cork might
also be full of unsuspected drama. When the final curtain fell in
the Cork Opera House, that wet night in 1915, I was ready to
explore, to respond to, for the first time to *see* the actuality of
life in Ireland.

To go back to the Young Irelanders, they were, then, wise
to encourage Irish writers to work on native material. Their
weakness was to have subserved literature to opinions, to political dogmatizing, to nationalist 'right' and 'wrong'. All would
have been fine had they gone on from the national-moral to
the universal-moral. Their sole concern was the purely local and
temporal. They could not have led the way to a Stendhal or a
Balzac. They led the way only to propaganda, as high-minded
and high-hearted as the songs and essays of early Garibaldians.
They had, however, one very important, ultimate influence on
Irish letters. They helped to inspire, among others, old John
O'Leary, the rebel Fenian, who in turn helped to inspire young
Yeats to stop writing about Morocco.

The development of modern Irish literature since the 1840s
might thus be described as a prolonged voyage of discovery,
conducted by Irish writers, into the common reality of Irish
life, present and past. As their intimacy with their material grew
their absorption grew with it. Sometimes they were delighted
by what they found, sometimes repelled, always they were ex-
cited, for the nationalist spirit was always at hand to excite
them, even if it were only to excite them to furious disagreements. This is the essential. Without the national thing – at any
rate up to our own day – an Irish writer was always in danger
of becoming a provincial by becoming an imitator. He would

not merely take models from other countries, Russia, France, or Germany, learn his trade from them, and apply himself then to his own sort of life which he knew so well: he would, if he remained an imitator, be a man of another country, describe the life of another country, and so inevitably fail. The national thing gave Irish writers the necessary resolution to find in the reality of Irish life the stuff of their work.

It sounds easy. It is, nevertheless, a curious thing about modern Irish literature that it has produced so few feet-on-the-ground realistic novels: perhaps not more than nine or ten – Maria Edgeworth's *Castle Rackrent*; Charles Kickham's *Knockagow*; William Carleton's *Fardorougha the Miser*, which is really romantic-realistic; the homely *Loughsiders* of that almost forgotten novelist Shan Bullock; George Moore's *Muslin* and, debateably, his *The Lake*; that superb novel by Somerville and Ross *The Real Charlotte*; Peadar O'Donnell's *Adrigoole*; Liam O'Flaherty's *The Informer*; Elizabeth Bowen's only Irish novel, as solid as it is beautiful, *The Last September*, and, of course, Joyce's *Portrait* and *Ulysses*.

It is equally significant that, with the exception of O'Flaherty and Joyce, all these novelists, and indeed the greater number of all Irish writers in prose, verse and drama, deal with *rural* life. We are not, basically, an urbanized country. We have no great industrial complexes. Our few cities, none of them large, lead the lives of big county towns. The main effect on our literature is that it is not, as yet, intellectually sophisticated.* To take extreme examples, an Anouilh, a Sartre or a Montherlant would be unthinkable in Dublin. I feel certain that there is a close connexion between the two things: realism and thought are inseparable. No realistic writer can expand beyond a merely descriptive local naturalism, can universalize his subject until he knows it not merely with his senses but with his intellect. When the thing ceases to exist for him in impersonal isolation it becomes part of his whole life as a man passionately pondering on the entire human condition. He will not then pass cold judgements or moralize explicitly – either would be a great

---

*I refer the reader back again to my reference (pages 54ff.) to the traditional anti-intellectualism of the Irish mind from the beginnings of its history.

bore — but he will quietly, even imperceptibly provoke his readers towards that end. It is what all the greater novelists do. We Irish do not, so far, ponder deeply or write realistically.

Which brings us naturally to Yeats and Joyce; the bell-wether of all our romantics and our one great realist. They help us to measure Ireland's achievement in this final stage of her long search for intellectual and imaginative freedom. With these two writers we may link in our minds the far less romantic Synge and the far less realistic O'Casey, for what these four writers did between them was to establish at last a new type of Irishman — the Irish-European.

How, today, would Irish literature rank without those four men of genius? We must bear in mind that between the Young Irelanders (of the 1840s) and Yeats (born in 1865, arriving at his maturity somewhere between 1910 and 1920) there had been many poets; Mangan, Allingham, Graves, Rolleston, Todhunter, Moira O'Neill, Lawless, Katherine Tynan and others who properly appear in every anthology of Irish poetry; all were reputable poets but none of them had anything approaching the genius and stature of Yeats. With him and after him there came other poets, incomparably better than any of those progenitors, yet still not of his stature. The same might be said of the progenitors and contemporaries of Synge and O'Casey in the theatre. The novel had a somewhat longer and more distinguished history. But, whether we are thinking of poetry, of drama, or of the novel, Irish literature without the Big Four would be now regarded throughout the world as no more and no less than an interesting regionalist literature. These four writers did what, in different ways, Georg Brandes, Ibsen, Björnson and Strindberg did for their capitals. They made Dublin a European literary centre.

They did not do it alone. Whitman once said in tribute to journalism that it forms the compost of literature; presumably all sorts of things are ecologically just as necessary to make a literature possible, such as the climate of its life and its history. In Ireland Anglo-Irish literature rose out of the ancestral memory, the painful political struggles of centuries, the admixture of blood and talent brought in by a long procession of ruthless colonists and conquerors, the intellectual blood transfusion resulting from the outflow and backtrack of constant expatriation, the imposition on Gaelic Ireland of the English language and the example of its masterpieces, the one offering to Irish writers access to the widest audience and the other access to a thousand shades of style. To the patriot this must seem a list of Grecian gifts presented as blessings. To the historian they are both. It is how all history happens. Take expatriation, or emigration. We would not now be able to claim Swift as in any sense an Irish writer if he had not at first had to leave Dublin for London and then, at the height of his powers, been shanghaied back from London to Dublin. As children we might never have been moved by the poverty, sadness and humour of Auburn if Goldsmith had not been exiled by his own poverty from Lissoy to Grub Street. We would have had no George Moore if the breakdown of the savage landlordism that produced him had not driven him from Mayo to Paris – from which Yeats's ancestral memory brought him back to Dublin. As our prime expatriate Joyce drily put it, the shortest way to Tara is via the mail-boat to Holyhead.

Yeats is a good example of the manner in which all those influences worked on Irish literature. To begin with, he spent almost half his life out of Ireland. As an infant he was in Dublin for three years. After that up to the age of fifteen he lived in London. Between fifteen and twenty-two he spent seven formative years in Dublin. There then followed fifteen years in London during which he published his first volumes of verse and wrote a number of oracular essays. Further residence in London, Oxford and Shillingford (after his marriage), visits to places like Sicily and Algeciras, and several winters spent on the Riviera account for another six or seven years, adding up in all to some thirty-four years of expatriation out of a life span of seventy-four.

Nobody can doubt that, despite these wanderings, he was most profoundly influenced by those early seven years in Dublin, and by his frequent visits to his beloved Sligo and to Clare-Galway. It is equally evident, however, that those thirty-four years or so that he spent mainly in London also left their mark on his intellect – not the happiest mark, as anyone may clearly see in the weary, attenuated, passionless and vague style both of his prose and verse during those years of expatriation: a style of writing, feeling and seeing more suited to a Beardsley or a Rosetti than to a young man from Dublin and Sligo. But when one thinks of his Rhymers' Club companions in the London of the eighties and nineties – Dowson, Johnson, Beardsley, Henley – one is not surprised that he and they should have been crudely told by the only one of the lot who had any real warmth or strength in his work, that what they all lacked was 'blood and guts'. I mean John Davison, the author of such fine poems as *In Romney Marsh* and *Thirty Bob a Week*, to whose influence on himself T. S. Eliot more than once paid grateful tribute.

It was not until he left London in 1902 that Yeats began, but only began, not exactly to free his intellect from those influences – for they too are part of his making – but to purify them by what Joyce called 'the shock of new material' – more Sligo, the Abbey Theatre, peasant plays, and so forth: the same medicine he had prescribed to Moore and Synge. That was the year when, aged thirty-seven, he had his famous first meeting with Joyce, then aged twenty, who upbraided him for what Wordsworth called his 'meddling intellect', for occupying himself with ideas and generalizations instead of seeking only the immediacy and concreteness proper to the artist.* But every man has his own maggot and Yeats's maggot was his simultaneous love for, and hatred of, ideas and generalizations; and it was largely because of this weakness that his influence on Irish letters was so long delayed and, to the end, remains more than dubious.

It is commonly thought that Yeats began to establish an influence on Irish letters soon after he returned to Dublin in 1902 and began his work in the Abbey Theatre. (It opened its doors in 1904.) The truth is quite otherwise. In the theatre he faced almost from the start frequent, savage and stupid opposition from his nationalist, Sinn Fein and Catholic critics. The religious attacks on his own *Countess Cathleen* and the nationalist riots over *The Playboy* are outstanding examples. Even as a poet he took a long time to win not merely the approval of the public but of his own fellow-writers. In fact, oddly enough, they

* It is one of the most fascinating of literary confrontations. For the full story see *Eminent Domain*, by Richard Ellmann, p. 37, Oxford, 1967.

far preferred the sort of poetry he had written before he came back to live in Dublin. In 1907, when he was forty-two, preparing his first collected volume of poems and beginning to emerge from his Celtic Twilight, we find George Moore declaring bluntly that his 'inspiration was declining', adding characteristically, 'We were not really sorry,' and reporting that Yeats's closest friend and fellow-poet AE also considered that he had written his best work. 'He would,' AE said, 'have written volume after volume if he had never sought a style, if he had begun to write simply.' It was a supremely silly observation, but it was made; and if Yeats's friends could say things like that we may guess what his enemies could do. He had exchanged a great metropolis for Dublin's *petit capital*, with its nationalist prejudices, its adoration of internecine controversies, its Lilliputian squabbles, its fatal genius for cynical mockery, all those provincial limitations that once made him speak of Ireland's 'great hatred, little room', of Dublin as 'this rude, unmannerly town'. He would, to be sure, have his public victories – as in his defence of Synge. He could always strike home with one of his 'occasional' poems, *At Galway Races*, or *At The Abbey Theatre*. But to see him as an established influence we have to wait until as late as the 1920s when his stature as a man and a poet could no longer be denied. As the novelist Peadar O'Donnell was to observe later, life in Ireland for any writer is always life in a cold climate.

Even after then it is a moot question whether – apart from his splendid, constant and haughtily fearless public insistence on the dignity and importance of the arts – he ever had any direct influence on Irish writing. There are three reasons for this. He had learned one hard lesson from the Rhymers: in their private lives they could be dissolute and undisciplined – Johnson an alcoholic, Dowson a chaser of waitresses, Richard le Gallienne a gay libertine, Davison a suicide – but their social lives as poets among poets were reticent and reserved. They taught him to be ceremonious, polite and aloof. In Dublin he cultivated distance. He had to! The second reason was that his mind was not, as I will show, an intellectual mind, a communicating mind. And, for all his incurable love of ideas, he was – in his Kantian insistence on the ineluctable limits of Reason as compared with the penetrating power of the Imagination – far more interested in the insubstantial world of his dreams than in the actual world of nature. This quality alone made it more than difficult for him to communicate with a Roman Catholic people – nine-tenths of peasant origin – trained, after the manner of Aristotle and Aquinas, by their priests to establish themselves in the mortal present before taking off for the immortal future, rather than the other way round, as he did. So, he was read with delight, though chiefly in his Irish-local-national poems; he had many imitators; but his direct influence on Irish writing as a whole is another matter.

To say that Yeats was not an intellectual may seem a strange thing to say of a man who spent his whole life pondering on idea after idea, and who was frequently and passionately concerned about the function of the intellect in the arts. Yet, if one thinks over his whole *œuvre*, prose, verse and drama, it is apparent that what he possessed, or that what possessed him, was not so much an intellect as a powerful and ever-questing imagination roving enthusiastically from one idea, or theory, or concept to another, giving to each only so much credence as would inspire a poem, or a series of poems – each of which poems could, by its eloquence and art, persuade the reader to believe that he was utterly committed to whatever idea he happened to be developing for the time being.

The truth is that Yeats had not a single idea in his head; he had thousands; all fighting one another, as the pursuing reader of his poems soon discovers on noting how often he will discard whatever idea possessed him so forcefully the year before in favour of another, often cognate, idea, again expressed with equal force. This is why Richard Ellmann, although his most sympathetic critic and most ingenious *advocatus angeli*, is driven to admit that although his work 'abounds in challenging statements about the world ... how sympathetically these are to be taken by the reader, and how firmly they are asserted by the writer, are problems that have vexed his critics'.

As Mr Stephen Spender has put it in *The Destructive Element*, the reader 'is at every stage perplexed'. He finds himself reading of mystery and twilight, and feels that he must be hushed and silent lest he disturb the fairy world. To his disappointment

he presently finds that the faery song is growing fainter and
fainter until, finally, it disappears over the crest of a twilit
hill; whereupon the reader realizes that all that faery poetry
had merely been part of a theory for developing folk-material
into sophisticated literature. 'But Yeats has not disappeared.
... On the contrary the fairies now merge into a theory of
Magic.' The magic in turn soon begins to fade. Was it genuine?
Was it just atmospherics? Was it symbolism? The poet's ambiguity becomes complete when the reader finds that the result of
the poet's search for one symbol has been 'the discovery that
almost anything might become that symbol'. And so on. Mr
Spender's most penetrating observation is that Yeats's rhetoric
always finely illustrates his thought but never develops it.
There is, indeed, he points out, especially in the later poems, a
great 'show of intellectualism'. The thought itself is 'hopelessly
inadequate to the situation'.

It should go without saying that no modern reader expects
for a moment that any poet must mean literally what he is saying symbolically; and we do not expect this of Yeats, any more
than we expect Shelley to have positively believed that his sky-
lark never was a bird, or Keats to have believed that his night-
ingale would never die. The trouble with so many of Yeats's
ideas is that they are, or seem to be presented to us as positive
beliefs. How else, for instance, are we to take these remarkable
lines, in his splendid poem *The Tower*:

> And I declare my faith:
> I mock Plotinus' thought
> And cry in Plato's teeth,
> Death and life were not
> Till man made up the whole,
> Made lock, stock and barrel
> Out of his bitter soul,
> Aye, sun, moon and star, all,
> And further add to that
> That, being dead, we rise,
> Dream, and so create translunar Paradise.

Ellmann's way of dealing with these declarations is to insist
that it is no answer to them to say that they are philosophical non-
sense. In these declarations, he says, 'Yeats is not maintaining

the position as a philosopher. He is simply uttering them out of an obstinacy which he wishes to be as mulish and heroic as he can make it.' He is, in other words, simply using Plato as a whipping boy because, in a sudden rush of humanism – which was, in any case, always at war in him with his own transcendence – he felt that Plato was 'all transcendence'. Later, possibly realizing that in his excitement he had fallen into a pit of subjectivism, or being perhaps simply in a cooler frame of mind, he was to admit that the designation did not really fit his enemy of the moment.

Today, as we read Yeats over and over again, from cover to cover, we easily take these variations or divagations in our stride. If anything they add to the delight of the poetry the fascination of reading the autobiography of a man who had to change in order to develop. Read in this way, or so it seems to me, his poetry flowers so movingly that any restless feelings we may have had about his inconsistencies vanish in our fascination with a search that never ended. It has been said of him, most aptly in one sense, that his end magnificently justified his beginnings. There is, in fact, no end. There could be none for so insatiable an explorer.

If his readers are Irish writers his work has the additional interest that wherever those beginnings were, wherever his flight took off, from Dublin, London or Sligo, his course was as wide as the universe. For while it is true that he held, after he discovered Ireland, that, 'To the greater poets, everything they see has its relation to the national life . . .', he went on, firmly, '. . . and through that to the universal and divine life. There is unity everywhere.' But if this is how we understand him now, it was hard, if not impossible to understand him while he was in the midst of his labyrinth. In AE's words many of his readers may have wished that he had written more simply. It was not in his nature, indeed not within his power, to compose otherwise than as an oracle, writing sybilline books. But neither can I go along with Mr Spender when he looked at the romantic Yeatsian façade and asked why was it necessary, or why does it not falsify the whole effect, and answered that 'Yeats's poetry is devoid of any unifying moral subject, and it develops in a perpetual search for one . . .' I should have thought that any purely ethical sense would have killed Yeats's natural genius stone dead. I can agree that Yeats 'offers no philosophy of life', but when Spender says that the magical system (which he substitutes for it) 'is not socially constructive' we are, I feel, thinking of a completely different kind of poet. It is right to say that Spender wrote this in the thirties, when poetry in England was more deeply than ever before or since concerned with the moral and social conscience. It was difficult for any critic at that period to understand – even with the example of D. H. Lawrence before them – that genius can also thrive on hokum.

Yeats had one other weakness which came between him and his immediate Irish successors. These were mostly writers of novels and stories, all observation, all eyes, avid for realism (even if they were never to achieve it), preoccupied with what Stendhal called 'the little actual facts' – those details and precisions which accumulate as well-imagined reality. In their sense, Yeats did not have an observing eye. He could evoke like a magician; he could not draw a picture. (I do not know if it matters in practice, but he was quite short-sighted.) See for instance his fine evocation of All Souls' Night, in Oxford:

> Midnight has come, and the great Christ Church Bell
> And many a lesser bell sound through the room;
> And it is All Souls' Night,
> And two long glasses brimmed with muscatel
> Bubble upon the table . . .

It is as near as he ever comes to the actual-pictorial, pleasing the prose writer by the image of the two slim glasses of bubbling wine, one for himself, one for the ghost. The prose writer is less pleased with the inexactness of the opening lines of *The Wild Swans at Coole*:

> The trees are in their autumn beauty,
> The woodland paths are dry.

But he is enchanted by the visual imagery of the next two lines,

> Under the October twilight the water
> Mirrors a still sky.

Yet he is never as delighted as he is with the precise evocation of Moore's lake that, when the white clouds were drawn about the earth, 'lay like a mirror that somebody had breathed on'. It is a matter of two needs, two approaches: the exiled poet eager to soar to his proper element with the souls of his dead friends on that November night; the novelist eager to give earth-place to his country-priest, already restless in a vocation that he will abandon with: 'There is a lake in every man's heart, and he listens to its monotonous whisper year by year, more and more attentive until at last he ungirds' — to swim across it to his human freedom.

The contrast with Joyce is apparent. He was far less imaginative. He was concrete, dry, cold-eyed, clear-headed and, though utterly rebellious against the gods, all-accepting towards man in a way and to a degree as far beyond the powers as it was beyond the desires of his great romantic contemporary. He was a realist with his feet planted on the ground, or, if one wishes to say so, in the gutter. (Yeats, too, had as a young man descended to the gutter, in his case the gutter of Irish politics that had no least interest for Joyce; but he moved among them with his head in the air and he soon left them in an understandable disgust.) The contrast is not, however, complete. To say that Joyce was less imaginative than Yeats or that he had his feet on the ground does not mean that he had not his own kind of imagination or that he could not soar. After all, he named his hero after that legendary artificer who not only invented the labyrinth of Minos, and the base device that enabled Queen Pasiphae to satisfy her bestial desires, but also the wings that soared Icarus to the sun. The vital difference between the two is one of emphasis, the poet reaching for the transcendent element, the novelist insisting on the human. Yeats, if pressed hard enough, would always underwrite the human to arrive at the transcendent. Joyce refused absolutely to underwrite anything in mortal life. Yeats, a born dualist, always hating his duality, always trying to resolve it, could say, 'There is Unity everywhere', but he did not mean his 'everywhere'. For him there were everywhere things that were divided, Body and Soul, the Beautiful and the Ugly, the Reason and the Imagination, and he perpetually wavering between them. Joyce (I quote the American critic and philosopher, William Barrett) insisted on holding all seeming opposites together, so that 'the spiritual premise of his work is an acceptance of life that no dualism, whether puritanical or aesthetic, could ever possibly embrace'. Here, surely, if anywhere in the course of modern Irish literature was a writer offering at least one coherent and liberating idea to the generation emerging after Yeats, if they really wanted intellectual and imaginative freedom from the pagan swaddling clothes of their country's infancy and the small-clothes of its over-prolonged Christian adolescence.

Unfortunately the generation of and after Yeats did not hear or heed Joyce. He came at a bad time. *A Portrait of the Artist* appeared in 1916. It was the year of the Rising which sparked off the Troubles that for some six years and more kept a generation of young men otherwise engaged. *Ulysses* appeared in 1922 on the verge of a Civil War whose horrors succeeded the Troubles, continued sporadically until 1924, and whose political rancours persisted years after the guns became silent. By the time that generation of writers was able to consider *Ulysses*, able even to buy the book, for it was not on open sale in holy Ireland until a few years ago, most of them – still warm with revolutionary ardour and idealism, however disillusioned by the comparison between old dreams and present realities – could only have been repelled by it: not because of Blazes Boylan's or Leopold Bloom's sensual passions for Molly Bloom or for Gerty MacDowell, but because of Joyce's olympian indifference to the charms of Cathleen ni Houlihan. Even if Joyce had been angry about Cathleen they could have understood, indeed, in their disillusion, been highly pleased. But to find that he was merely amused by their goddess was too much! 'Does anybody in Ireland read *Ulysses*?' Joyce asked Beckett soon after the book appeared. Beckett was able to mention a few names. 'But,' Joyce observed, 'they are all Jews!' On the other hand we were all soaked in romantic Yeats, meaning poems like *Easter 1916*, *On a Political Prisoner*, *Sixteen Dead Men*, *Meditations in Time of Civil War*, or *Nineteen Hundred and Nineteen*. By the time Joyce was being widely read by the 1920–50 generation – read, that is, in the full sense of reading and rereading him, mentally digesting him, retailing favourite bits of his works, delighting in his ruthless veracity, his sub-surface humour, his incomparable command of words, his bird-like eye, his unforgettably graphic phrases, we were already set. Too old to be influenced by him?

In a sentence, then, despite everything that had happened in Ireland since 1916, rebellion, revolution, civil war, even their bitter price in the death of friends and the disillusion of the living, Irish writing after Yeats did not clearly take, or give, the measure of the winds of change. However they might think of themselves, and many thought themselves tough realists, ruthless satirists, or even (Heaven help us!) keen intellectuals, Irish writers remained *au fond* incurably local and romantic.

Nowadays I sometimes say, to tease my fellows, 'You are all men of the twenties.' Their eyes glow, recalling our glorious twenties. 'I mean,' I add, 'of the eighteen-twenties' – as Yeats (Shelley and all that) was until his dying day. Not that, with one proviso, there is anything wrong with being romantic, as Yeats proved. The proviso is whether the world about us will play ball with our romanticism. Otherwise it is like playing tennis with a ghost. Yeats was so lucky! He had the Irish folk-world, now taken over by tourism and T.V.; Irish mythology and hagiology, now, and none too soon, in the hands of the sceptical scholars; Symbolism, long since taken over by Freud, set to work in literature by Joyce; Indian philosophy, a dateable vogue; Magic, now the fieldwork of anthropologists, historians and philosophers like Lévi-Strauss or Marcia Eliade, or commercialized by glossy periodicals like *Planète* to comfort the faithless French; Spiritualism, Madame Blavatsky, Rosicrucianism, table-rapping 'and all that lark' as Brendan Behan used to say (How on earth did Yeats ever manage to turn all that lark into such fine poetry?) and he had, so inspiringly, the revolutionary fight for liberty, long since de-romanticized by the invention of total war, the horrors of Algeria, Cyprus, Israel, the Congo, Vietnam, Nigeria ...

In his last poem Yeats unrepentantly told us how and what to write if we wished to be 'still the indomitable Irishry'. We were to sing of peasants, hard-riding country gentlemen, the holiness of monks, porter-drinkers' laughter, and

> Sing the lords and ladies gay
> That were beaten into the clay
> Through seven heroic centuries ...

Yet, with that characteristic honesty which was his ultimate non-commitment, he had in the preceding lines on the *quattrocento* acknowledged the impossibility of doing just this.

> Gyres run on;
> When the greater dream was gone
> Calvert and Wilson, Blake and Claude
> Prepared a rest for the people of God,
> Palmer's phrase, but after that
> Confusion fell upon our thought.

After that he wrote his epitaph, bidding us all to cast a cold eye on life, on death. Not an easy man to please! And, yet, he was, on the whole, pleased with us, pleased enough at least to gather some of us into the Academy of Letters that he founded in 1932 with the help of the highly sceptical Shaw.*

Looking back now at 1920–50 my most profound regret is that it had not been possible for us all to have read cold Joyce in our warm teens. For after Yeats this green corner of the universe refused any longer to play romantic ball. Ireland ceased to be a romantic island. We had needed the colder guide.

In the most creative fifty years of Anglo-Irish literature then

---

* Writing to me in October 1940, when I was Honorary Secretary of the Academy, Shaw said: 'Yeats could have been under no delusion as to my opinion of the project; and I did nothing but draft a constitution, the only really important clause in which was designed to avoid fossilization.' (He was referring to an age-average clause.) 'Of course they threw that clause out at the first opportunity . . .' (He then goes on to recall his earlier disillusioning experiences with an English Academy founded as a Committee of the Royal Society of Literature; its blackballing of Hilaire Belloc; its average committee-age of 77; its inevitable future when 'self-elected dotards like myself' would die of old age.) 'With this experience you may imagine what I thought of Yeats's scheme. Still, I approve of academics and national theatres and the like as public monuments to the importance of literature and the drama, even if they are as inert as public statues and happily less visible.' The rest of his remarks are ruderies about the Catholic University at Maynooth, Trinity College and the Irish censorship. But he may have been a little out of touch. One of his queries was, 'Does Maynooth still exist?' *Does* it!

(from about 1890 to about 1940) the writers saw Irish life, in the main, romantically. It was as a poetic people that they first introduced themselves to the world, and it is as a poetic people that we are still mainly known abroad. The peasant-plays of the Abbey Theatre, even when supposedly realistic, held still the charm of external novelty – dress, speech, situation, humour – and were bathed in that sense of natural wonder which is best illustrated by the plays of Synge. Towards the end of the period a satirical note made itself felt, and in the plays of Sean O'Casey – all the natural wonder being removed, for they are set in the Dublin slums – we were left with an assuaged realism. The Novel, budding from the work of George Moore and James Joyce, and profoundly affected by the French and Russian realists, likewise began to hold a far from indulgent mirror up to nature. When the revolutionary period of 1916–22 ended miserably in a civil war, romance began to wilt. Much Irish literature since 1922 has been of an uncompromising scepticism, one might sometimes even say ferocity. I need quote but one example, the novels of Liam O'Flaherty.

Once the people began to see themselves in these various lights it could only be a matter of time before they became intellectually and imaginatively free – free of their own feeble or flattering self-opinions, free of all sorts of assumptions about themselves, native or foreign; free of easy assumptions about others. But this experience could hardly be painless, and the process is far from finished. It is a matter of record that the Irish theatre has probably seen more riots than any other; and it is probable that, between 1929 and, say, 1955, a greater proportion of native writers of note were banned in Ireland than in Russia.

What has, for the moment, happened is that which I mentioned at the close of the chapter on 'The New Peasantry' (p. 84). The Irish people have entered into the last stage of that process of urbanization which began when the Norman invasion sowed towns and town-life all over a mainly pastoral country. From the very beginning of our history this is a process which we have resisted. Even now we resist it still. We are rooted in the land and in individualism. We have always feared towns. We have felt them as spear-heads of life-ways which are complex, troublesome and challenging. Today we call those life-ways 'foreign' and in trying to impose a peasant life-way on the towns we try to exclude anything which the 'peasant' (especially the Catholic peasant) does not understand. Literature is, naturally, one of those things which the 'peasant' looks upon with the greatest suspicion. That the poor fellow's defences are meanwhile being utterly undermined by the vulgarities of the cinema, the radio, trashy books, cheap amusements, 'foreign' fashions of every sort, and the chase for easy money, and by the effects of a hand-over-fist emigration to industrial Britain under the worst social conditions, he does not realize in the least. He thinks himself safe behind a formal religion and an emotional Nationalism that is, at least, a century out of date.

To see why this should all be so – why, especially, our Nationalism, which was so fructive politically from O'Connell onward, should no longer be viable – we must turn to the sixth and last branch of the growing tree of Irish life: our politicians.

13

THE POLITICIANS

LITTLE though they know it, the dominating problem for all Irish politicians, ever since the founding of the Free State, has been what to do with their lovely Past. ('O lost, and by the wind grieved, ghost come back again!') They are not the only people in a like dilemma. A painter friend living in Switzerland tells me that a common and anxious question today among thoughtful Swiss is, 'We have everything! But where on earth has William Tell gone to?' We Irish could tell them. He is probably managing a factory in Kerry or Tipperary, side by side with our Cuchulainn, and a large number of hard-worked and hard-headed Irishmen, and a number of other foreigners, American, English, German, Belgian, Dutch, Japanese, Canadian, French. But whatever they are manufacturing one thing is certain: it is nothing to do with the Past. This change from more spectacular forms of revolutionary activity began slowly and tentatively. It did not really accelerate properly until the sons, in some cases even the grandsons of the men and women of the generation of 1916 set out, in earnest, to make liberty viable in terms of the modern commercial and industrial world.

It is a process that has not been universally approved. No sooner had it started than some people, more traditionally minded than others, began to ask the Swiss question. Others, like the young men of the IRA went on for years blowing up things in the middle of the night – the Nelson Pillar did not go until 1966 – to show that the glorious traditions of liberty still live on untarnished. But the favourite butt of all traditionalists was the man in charge of Change – the politician. For while everybody in Ireland wanted efficiency and modernization, everybody also wanted to preserve the old folk-ways and the old folk-values that had been our laws of life for centuries. 'Frugal Comfort!' said Mr de Valera, thinking of his boyhood. 'Sports cars!' said the young men, thinking of theirs.

The ambivalence was deep; the conflict widespread and lasting.

Indeed, nobody clung more devotedly to the old pieties than our first generation of would-be modernizers; unless it be our churchmen, who always cling to the past as lovingly as the ivy that chokes the growing tree. Once, being as bewildered as anybody else about what we really wanted, I begged one of our early administrators to reveal to me his ideal image of the new Ireland that he was so ardently toiling to create. 'I want,' he said, with all the energy of a newborn realist, 'an Ireland like Sweden! But,' he added, with all the passion of an insuppressible idealist, 'it must be an Ireland with all the old Irish ways!' A thoughtful Swiss, or Swede, might sigh. An Irish past-worshipper might think of (but tactfully not utter) Yeats's verse:

> Toil and grow rich
> What's that but to lie
> With a foul witch,
> And after, drained dry,
> To be brought to the chamber where
> Lies one long sought
> With despair?

Realism versus Idealism. New Wealth rather than old Virtue. Past or Future? Progress or Stasis? Bang! Bang! Bang! The history of all post-revolutionary periods is loud with this kind of controversial gunshot.

The fact is that very few, if any of us, in the new Ireland realized how many of the old ways would have to die if a new Ireland was ever to grow to full strength. Yet, the passing of the past was surely inevitable? Over thirty years ago, Robin Flower – then Keeper of Manuscripts in the British Museum, a devoted lover of the Great Blasket Island, where he had gathered, in Gaelic, scores of folk tales as old as Greece – told me that he already foresaw the end of the old ways one night when he sat among a group of islanders before the turf-fire, with the Atlantic storm whining under the door and howling down the chimney, at the moment when one of the men, instead of saying as usual, 'Inis scéal eile dhúinn, a Michíl,' (Tell us another story, Michael), pulled out a newspaper, turned to a small schoolboy sitting amongst the group and asked him to translate the news from Dublin. It reminds me forcibly of something Shaw said to me about Ayot St Lawrence, then in the untrodden wilds of Hertfordshire. 'When I came here,' he said in that fine Irish brogue that he never lost, 'this place was in the Middle Ages. One day, the postmistress bought a radio and overnight the village was in the twentieth century.' Time was to prove Robin Flower right. The Great Blasket Island is now a deserted rock: its girls simply refused to marry any longer within the island.

These long and far from intelligent doubts and irresolutions of ours about the Past and the Future, that have bedevilled Irish political thinking for fifty years and more, seem to me to show that the basic trouble with our politicians is that with quite notable exceptions,* they have never paused to consider the true meaning of the word Culture. Instead of thinking of it as an all-inclusive way of life, which often takes centuries to construct, they keep on thinking of it as a bonus stuck like a stamp on the envelope of life. To them culture is a picture on the wall, a book on a shelf, a symphony orchestra, a new theatre building, a new convention-hall, something always midway between a private possession and a useful, state-sponsored tourist-attraction.

Here, by contrast, is T. S. Eliot's list of some of the manifold characteristics of the culture of his adopted country: 'Derby Day, Henley Regatta, Cowes, the Twelfth of August, a cup final, the dog races, a pin table, Wensleydale cheese, boiled cabbage cut in sections, beetroot in vinegar, the dart board, nineteenth-century Gothic churches and the music of Elgar.'† One observes that Eliot puts music last, and that it is his only instance of what our people and politicians still think of as culture. He does so because he is thinking of culture not as something imposed upon life but as an intrinsic part of life. He is thinking of it socially, in terms of a people who have been projecting, visibly, tactually, audibly and edibly, over the centuries, their racial genius for living. It is no doubt hard for politicians to think in this way, in any country. Pragmatists and empiricists

---

*I am thinking of such exceptional politicians as Dr Noel Browne, Eoin Ryan and Senator Garret Fitzgerald.

†*Notes Towards a Definition of Culture*, p. 31, London, 1938.

to a man, they would have to be visionaries, prophets, even poets before they could realize that what they are supposed to be doing is not alone to be nursing the economy of their country but to be doing so in order the better to nurture an entire, and for us Irish an almost entirely new, desirable pattern of living. If they are not doing this they might just as well be managing a dry-goods store in Brooklyn.

It was particularly hard for our first politicians, after 1922, to think in this way because they laboured under one terrible disadvantage: they had practically no social-minded predecessors to guide them. I can think of only two: Michael Davitt (1846–1906), the founder of the Land League to liberate the peasant farmers from the inhuman poverty of their lives; and James Connolly, the labour leader and founder of The Irish Citizen Army, who was executed in 1916. Otherwise our past political leaders spoke or wrote loftily only in terms of what used to be vaguely called The National Faith; but they never defined it in terms of a desirable image of what life would look like and feel like in a free Ireland. At most they thought, like all our politicians since, of how to improve Irish subsistence conditions; which is not, of course the same thing at all as improving the aesthetic, moral and intellectual level of life. It is a simple but vital distinction not lost on politicians but surprisingly often overlooked by them in the stress of trying to keep the ship of state afloat at all.*

The reason why, apart from the land-war, Irish Nationalism in the nineteenth and early twentieth century was lacking in social content is simple. The backbone of all nationalist politics since Daniel O'Connell (1775–1847) was a semi-educated peasantry, led by a comparatively few men and women of the middleclasses and lower middleclasses mostly urbanized but also rarely more than a generation or two removed from the land. The immediate result was that our Nationalism, having no proletarian-industrial class in this mainly pastoral island to inject a social content into it, developed almost wholly as a mystique. Politics as the technology or blueprint of a new way of life, was beyond it. Davitt and Connolly apart, we produced no Bazarovs.

*For further amplification of this point see the Appendix.

A brief glance at our three major political groups today may throw some light on the ultimate results: beginning with the representatives of the workers.

Not until 1902 was there any talk of founding an Irish Labour Party – the British Labour Party had won its first two seats in the Commons in 1900 – but it was not until 1912 that the Irish Trades Union Congress gave instructions for the drafting of a constitution for such a party. Then came the great tramway lock-out of 1913 and Jim Larkin's militant socialism. The war followed, Larkin went to America, and to Sing Sing. Connolly took Larkin's place. The Irish Citizen Army was founded. Meanwhile, however, Sinn Fein was fast becoming active, the Irish Parliamentary Party in the Commons was fast losing power, and the Trades Unions, in the usual stolid, bureaucratic, apolitical way of all Trades Unions, went on consolidating – as unions. After Connolly was executed in 1916 the only one of these three groups that counted politically was nationalist Sinn Fein.

Gradually the middle-classes generally moved towards Sinn Fein, and this naturally tended to introduce an element of conservatism into Sinn Fein. The future of Ireland was now largely in the hands of Sinn Fein, and Sinn Fein was determined not to confuse the political struggle by becoming involved directly in any clash of social interests. ... Their task was made easier by the decision of Labour not to participate directly in the dramatic deliberations of the first Dáil.*

(That is, in the first, 1919, Sinn Fein, abstentionist, republican, and, from the British point of view wholly illegal, and therefore underground, though democratically elected parliament in Dublin.)

A brief and sketchy Democratic Programme for the free Ireland that was to come to pass three years later did emerge from this first gathering of republicans. (Labour took no part in these deliberations but two labour leaders did privately help to compose the first draft.) It was a slight document, consisting

* The above quotation is from the revealing essay, 'The Social Revolution that Never Was', in that useful volume *The Irish Struggle, 1916–1926*, edited by Desmond Williams. (London, 1966.) The essay is by Patrick Lynch. I am much indebted to it and, by his kind permission, use it freely in this section.

of less than five pages of print, in Irish and in English, and it was read, listened to and discussed for precisely twenty minutes and fifty seconds, and then buried forever. More than that, the original draft had been so watered down that it no longer contained such declarations as that 'it shall be the purpose of the Government to encourage the organization of the people into Trades Unions and cooperative societies with a view to the control and administration of industries by the workers'; or, that 'no private property is good as against the public right of the nation'. ('Words,' observes Lynch, 'ironically taken from Patrick Pearse, written in *The Sovereign People* of March 31st 1916. Pearse was already being expurgated.')

It may be fairly argued in defence of that first Dáil of 1919 that its members were outlaws who had no facilities and no time for intellectual discussions about life in the coming Ireland. But, it must surely also be asked, what of the intellectual leaders, such as the Labour Party, or that gallant agitator and main Sinn Fein propagandist, Arthur Griffith, later the first premier of the Free State? Just as Sinn Fein remained strictly asocial the Labour Party remained at this time strictly apolitical: it had not contested the elections which created that first Dáil of 1919, and it likewise cautiously held off from the elections of 1921 which produced the second Dáil and which ultimately voted on the Treaty that set up the new Free State. They did so 'in the belief,' says Lynch mildly, 'that by abstaining they were leaving the people free to express themselves unambiguously.' About their own freedom? He adds, less mildly: 'They committed themselves to an arid and ambiguous neutrality.' As for Arthur Griffith: 'Wherever Griffith saw socialist influence he sensed British influence. "The man," he wrote, "who injures Ireland, whether he does it in the name of Imperialism or Socialism is Ireland's enemy." ' The result, Lynch goes on, was that after political liberation was secured in 1922: 'The social conflict, as seen from Wolfe Tone to Connolly, and indeed by socialist republicans after him, had become submerged. . . . Labour, largely because of its own behaviour, presented no serious challenge to the economic or social philosophy of the Government. The role of Labour was now sectional or marginal, in no sense crucial or central.'

It was not until around 1967 that this situation began to change somewhat; when the Labour Party first dared to appear before the electors as a frankly socialist party. Nevertheless members of the Labour Party were, by 1968, adopting slogans and clichés that by then were being hastily discarded by socialists in many European countries as being fifty years out of date. They had, that is, closed their eyes to the fact that this repetition of weary bromides was obscuring the prime historical fact that both capitalism and socialism had meanwhile changed. The peaceful occupation of French factories by workers in 1968 might alone have shown them how far ahead of its time, as an interpretation of Marxism, the dynamic thought of their founding father James Connolly had been. The Trades Unions were thus just as reactionary as our private entrepreneurs in recognizing the powerful and distinctive role that public enterprise, i.e. well-managed semi-state bodies, could play in a mixed economy in reaching some of the economic and social objectives of the Democratic Programme of that first Dáil away back in 1919. In short, Irish Trades Unions have indeed improved the wages of their workers but they have done very little to change the shape of the society in which they live.

It is not necessary to speak at any length of the government party which took over power in 1922, and whose successors are the party now known as Fine Gael. For five years they were, for reasons to be dealt with in a moment, all powerful. For the first ten years of the Free State they were the sponsors of the form of society that was to set the broad pattern for Irish life ever since: one based on a philosophy of *laissez faire* qualified only, and happily, by the creation of such publicly owned enterprises as communications, radio, electricity, sugar and transport by air, rail and road, to compensate for the inadequacies and timidities of the new, native, acquisitive middle classes, whose social thinking proved to be no more than a simplified replica of the acquisitive society they displaced, and which Joyce has so contemptuously immortalized in his ruthless descriptions of life in Dublin around 1902. The views of this Party have undergone many changes and reformations since then, but the sad impression they made on all socially thinking republicans during their first, crucial ten years of power has proved hard to kill.

The third group, now called Fianna Fáil, deserves a little closer examination, since, from the start, or at least at the start of its career, it represented itself to the people as a party of social reform. To measure its quality and sincerity in this role we have to glance at the circumstances surrounding its origin.

Before the establishment of the Free State there was not a bookshop in Dublin whose shelves were not packed with books, widely exported and highly priced, about what had been known since Parnell as The Irish Question. After 1922 these books floated out to the book-barrows where one could buy for pence what had once cost pounds. The Irish Question was settled and the world was sick of it. But that the Question had never, in fact, been properly framed, or completely answered inside Ireland was quickly shown by a bitter if blessedly brief Civil War – if even ten months of fratricidal strife can ever be considered brief.*

This Civil War had a profound and lasting influence on all subsequent Irish politics. It arose because a strong minority of the people considered that the Treaty of 1922, which founded the Free State, was a dishonourable settlement if considered in the light of all our past traditions. The main objections to it were that it was a betrayal of the 1916 Declaration of an Irish Republic and of all it stood for, in so far as it accepted the partition of Ireland, permitted the presence of British naval bases on Irish soil, a governor general in Dublin representing the Crown, and, above all – the telling symbol – introduced an oath of allegiance to the Crown to be subscribed to by every member of the Dáil. More generally, it was felt, in the words of one of the most active leaders of the republican Resistance, Liam Mellows, that only 'the commercial interests and the merchants were on the side of the Treaty. *We* are back to Wolfe Tone, and it is just as well, relying on the men of no property.' In

---

*The Irish Civil War broke out on 28 June 1922, when the army of the Free State attacked the headquarters of the rebels of the Irish Republican Army in Dublin. On 30 April 1923 Mr de Valera for the rival Republican government, and Mr Frank Aiken, Chief of Staff for the rival Republican army ordered all fighting to stop. It had, in fact, stopped long before. Some ten thousand Republicans had, by then, been arrested and interned. During the war seventy-seven Republicans were executed by the Free State government.

short Mellows and his comrades felt that the whole thing was a betrayal of all our old political dreams, our primordial values, our ancestral memories, and the centuries-old struggle of the dispossessed poor against an exploiting empire. What on earth, Mellows and his comrades asked, had all those ancient traditions to do with oaths of allegiance to the head of the ancient enemy? He would rather die than take such an oath; and he did die, executed by his former comrades in arms who – according as one wishes to interpret their reasoning – more pragmatically, more hard-headedly or more cynically considered the oath and the other conditions embodied in the Treaty as mere formalities that would, in time, perhaps, be got rid of by a process of gradual attrition. (The formula of Michael Collins, and events have proved him right, was that the Treaty provided 'the freedom to achieve freedom'.)

Within a year of the defeat of the Republicans in the field they astonished the country by winning in 1923 in an open election, as a constitutional party, forty-four seats as against the Government's sixty-three, showing clearly either – we will never know which – how many people had always disliked the Treaty settlement, or how many disliked the social pattern of life already emerging, or how many were sick to death of violence, which continued sporadically for years. This Republican party – in Gaelic Fianna Fail, meaning soldiers of destiny – was, however, an abstentionist party, refusing to enter the traitors' Dáil at least for as long as that hateful oath of allegiance remained in force. This stalemate, entirely agreeable to the Free State government, lasted for about four years. Then, Mr de Valera, seeing that there was no political future for any abstentionist party, persuaded himself and his followers that the oath really was merely a meaningless formula, led his party into the Dáil where each man signed the book in which every member had to record that he was subscribing to the oath. (Mr de Valera said he signed it just as if doing no more than signing his autograph. Less, evidently, *is* more?) Five years later, in 1932, Fianna Fail won enough votes to give it power, with the support of the Labour Party, as the Government of the Irish Free State. Off and on since then (1932) the Fianna Fail party has been in power for over thirty years.

Of those first ten years of Republican impotence before and after the Civil War – five in the wilderness and five inside the Dáil; tirelessly struggling, impatiently waiting for success – the first five especially have left an indelible mark on Fianna Fail, still discernible in the public and private utterances of its older and more embittered politicians. They were years of deep-rooted memories of defeat, of humiliation and frustration for the men, of penury and hardship for their wives and families; years of temptation and longing, for revenge, for power, and, not to put a tooth in it, for some sort of steady income. One saw them on the hustings, in the streets, the same old 1916 idealists, 'at close of day ... among grey eighteenth-century houses', but not now 'coming with vivid faces from counter or desk', because these febrile, fractious, bitter, hungry-eyed ex-freedom-fighters were now in every sense out of a job; shabbily dressed, wearing old hats that one liked to think had once been grazed by bullets, their ankle-length overcoats stuffed with manifestoes and pamphlets, their mouths thin with enmity and resolve, and one guessed at empty pockets, perhaps even empty stomachs, and wondered how or on what, in God's name, they and theirs lived.

One heard them tell with twisted laughter of their efforts to keep the body alive for the soul's sake: of this man who spent his day in a cellar stirring a cauldron to manufacture saleable bars of household soap; of that man who spent his day tramping from one small shop to another trying to peddle whatever small things he had been able to gather enough shillings to invest in, from babies' rubber soothers to penny pencils; another man who was so amazingly lucky as to have small insurance policies to peddle among the veriest poor of the slums; another who composed advertising slogans on postcards (he could not afford stamps for letters), which he sent around to the new 'commercial interests and merchants' with a request for a modest guinea if his clever slogan were adopted; the wife who took in other people's washing; the girl, yet no longer a girl, a worker from her teens, still working and waiting loyally for her man. They reminded one at times of those exiled Russian revolutionaries of the sixties and seventies so often observed in the cafés and taverns of Geneva, Paris and London, still stubbornly conspiring like Michael Bakunin, still propagandizing like Alexander Herzen with his little rebel paper *The Bell*; except that some at least of those revolutionaries had private means, and their lives were lightened by the most complex and explosive love-affairs. These Irish idealists had only one mistress. Always at their backs they had the loving and inspiring memories of their dead comrades; always before them there shone the light of the promised land, the day when they would once more proclaim the living Republic and undo all the harm that had been done to the National faith by their faithless fellows. In those harsh years the iron entered into the souls of our nationalist Left. During forty years it never melted. It was too useful a lode, if only to stiffen their resolve to prove to their countrymen that they, who had been so often mocked as hair-splitters, dreamers and extremists, could, in power, manage Ireland's affairs as well or better than their traitorous predecessors.

Did they? They did. Just as well, sometimes better, and in exactly the same manner; partly because the way of life of 'the merchants and the commercial interests' was by now too well entrenched to be uprooted easily; partly because once in power they became cagey; but mainly because their blazing mystique still had no social content. It was as if every man Jack of them had read and noted the words of John Galsworthy's character who said: 'There is just one rule for politicians all over the world. Don't say in Power what you say in Opposition. If you do you will only have to carry out what the other fellows found impossible.'

On the credit side, and it is much to their credit, and especially to the credit of Mr de Valera, (though even here the way had been paved for them by their predecessors' work in helping to establish the co-equal relationship of the Dominions inside the British Commonwealth, and the right of every parliament to repeal or amend every existing Act of Parliament) they did, bit by bit, legislate the Oath and the governor general out of existence; and they ultimately even got rid of the British naval bases. They also did much to accelerate the development of Irish industries, if still mainly on a small scale, under a system of protective tariffs and quotas. On the debit side, by this very development, they naturally further entrenched the merchants and commercial classes, and did so little for the working classes that emigration reached new heights; though, in full justice, it has to be said that after 1932 the de Valera housing programme for the workers was one of the most progressive in Europe, and removed some of the worst urban slums to be then found in any civilized society. About partition the party could do nothing – nobody could. And they never did declare their living Republic – Mr de Valera wrongly fearing, as events proved, that Ireland's commercial ties with Great Britain would be endangered by so extreme an action, and that it would further antagonize Northern Ireland. In fact, ironically, it was the party which had originally founded the 'hated' Free State that finally, on returning to power under Mr John Costello in 1948, declared the Republic as we now have it. Alas, like the legacy of a rich uncle who lives on until his nephew is half dead from starvation before he gets it, gifts too long witheld lose their virtue. When the Republic was proclaimed every party welcomed it, the states of the world recognized it, the Church which had in 1922 condemned to the point of excommunication those who fought for it, now blessed it, some poor, dead bones may have stirred at the cannons' roar, and in no least degree did it alter any aspect of the pattern of life in Ireland.

But that restless ghost, our Past, still refused to go away. Unplacated, it had tauntingly pursued Fianna Fail for several years after they achieved power, under the shadowy name of the IRA. Haunted like Richard III by the ghosts they had deposed Fianna Fail treated them as they themselves had been treated in their own ghostly days. They imprisoned the ghost, starved it, executed it and apparently crushed it. With the war the ghost rose bloodily again, and sank again. It was again rustling around the pillows of Fianna Fail in the late fifties and early sixties. At what point and by whom it was decided that something must finally be done about our lovely and accursed Past it is now impossible to say, but done it was, and with the apparent agreement of all our political leaders, in a most interesting way.

Had our political oracles decided at any point ruthlessly to abandon all plans for re-establishing the old ways, the old values, the old pieties, if only in the name of modernization and progress, many Irishmen would undoubtedly have thought it the greatest betrayal since Judas. The Gaelic revivalists and the intransigent IRA would certainly have thought so. Others would have thought it the best thing left undone since the day before God made woman. Had our politicians set out ruthlessly to re-establish the old ways – such as, the Irish language – the traditionalists would have acclaimed it as the greatest revival since Lazarus. Others would have consoled themselves, as Einstein did about the atomic bomb, with the thought that even if half the population of Ireland was gassed there would still be enough books left, and enough men capable of thought, to bring civilization back again. The third alternative would have been that adopted by all developing countries, which is, cunningly, frankly and intelligently, to adapt old traditions to new circumstances. But this does mean hard work, as well as a very great deal of frankness and intelligence. 'Tradition,' says T. S. Eliot, 'cannot be inherited. If you want it you must obtain it, by great labour' – adding that, even so, it must then be perpetually criticized to keep it up to date. Which is obvious enough. After all, not even the most fanatical traditionalist would propose that all Irishmen should, in the name of tradition, wear kilts; or, as the old Celts often did, fight stark naked; or adopt the ancient Brehon Laws which, among other things, acknowledged polygamy; or that we should go on for ever living in nice, old, flea-ridden, thatched cottages and rear our hens in our kitchens.

As it happened our politicians adopted none of those alternatives. Instead, an entirely novel view of Irish history came into being, it is widely felt under the influence of Fianna Fail (those thirty years in power), and of Mr de Valera, whose thinking has always been lovingly rooted in the past, as well as dominated by a lawyer's belief that everything can be solved by an ingenious formula. According to this view of history nothing at all need be done about old traditions because they were, are and always would be virginal, perennial, omni-present and indestructible, their purity never in the least scathed by any one of those cross-breedings, vicissitudes or reformations that I have recorded in this book. Our culture, from the beginning to the end, was therefore held to be the perfect fruit of the continuous and uninterrupted development of an ancient Gaelic civilization. Once this engaging historical myth was accepted nobody need *do* anything about the past, except serenade its constant and effortless reincarnation. Indeed, nobody should try. Gods, not men, produce national metempsychosis. The upshot of it has been that the spirit of the Past is now widely regarded amongst us as a purely immaterial force pumping a million times a day in the rose-pink heart of every true Irishman.*

If this is myth-faking it is not without precedent. It is the very basis of Zionism. The Orient thrives on it. All the values by which the British Empire lived depended on the faking of history to clothe colonialism as liberation. Countless Africans need the myth of an unbroken past to give them national pride. One of the most charming examples of fake-myth as history is the idea brought back from exile by Louis XVIII that the French Revolution had been merely a vulgar 'breach in the natural and good order of things', the execution of king, queen, and thousands of aristocrats a mere temporary mental aberration that all true Frenchmen could henceforth forget.† Our Louis XVIII held, likewise, that the Conquest had been no more than an unmannerly interruption of our history; that our famous seven hundred years of slavery had accomplished nothing; and that nothing had happened in or to the republican vision of life since Pearse and his men died for it in 1916.

---

*Since I am writing this chapter at the end of a book devoted to a consideration, I trust sympathetic, of our past, I am not likely to be now thought of as deriding a devoted interest either in our past, or in its vital relation to our present and future development. I fully see the force of the Lévi-Strauss's question :–'Is it not the character of myths, which have such an important place in our research, to evoke a suppressed past and to apply it like a grid upon the present, in the hope of discovering a sense in which the two aspects of his own reality that man is confronted with – the historical and the structural – coincide?' What we are concerned with is the correct interpretation of the signs and symptoms of the past. Otherwise we do not get a myth at all from the past, but a fake-myth, and therefore, inevitably, a fake-present, a fake coincidence, in short a wrong set of conclusions. See *The Scope of Anthropology*: Inaugural Lecture, Chair of Social Anthropology, Collège de France, 5th January 1960. London, 1967. Paperback edition by Jonathan Cape.

† See *The French Nation*, by Sir Denis Brogan, London 1957. p. 21.

The 'real' Ireland was thus at last secure, safely embodied for ever in the words of a Constitution which Mr de Valera drew up, and which was passed by plebiscite, in 1937. And if anybody questioned this achievement he was answered with more words, as when, on a famous occasion, Mr de Valera brought the Oxford English Dictionary into the Dáil and read from it the authoritative definition of the Republic which he so steadfastly refused to proclaim, let alone to translate into terms of the common life of the common man. If anybody dared do more than question the authority of the great English philologist – and within a year of the passing of the Constitution the IRA was to break out, in England and in Ireland, into one of the most violent explosions in its history – he was promptly silenced in the ruthless manner aforesaid.

For anybody who has, without total disagreement, so far pursued this brief record of the growth of an ancient people towards political maturity as a modern people all this must point to one of the most sad and stagnant phases of our long struggle to recognize that, in every age, the past is but the twilight of the dawn. Sad it certainly was, and that it ended in a state of almost total political and economic stagnation is now admitted by all parties. If anybody wishes to evoke the inmost feelings of that melancholy period he might read the memoirs of our most vivid Republican rebel, Brendan Behan's *Borstal Boy* – banned under the pretext that it was indecent and obscene by government censorship – though they are all summed up by the moving curtain-line in the Abbey Theatre's excellent dramatization of his book at the point when Brendan arrives home in Dublin Bay after a spell of imprisonment in England. Greeted heartily by a Customs officer with, 'Ah, Brendan! It must be marvellous to feel free!' The returned exile pauses for a split second, says drily, 'Aye! It must!' and passes on into what I once heard him call our Paper Republic. Otherwise the stubborn refusal of a whole generation of young men to be fobbed off with words is now commemorated only in the rebel songs of our singing pubs.

That some degree of cynicism about politics and politicians should have been engendered by those melancholy years was no more than natural. Yet, if we merge those bad, sad years into the full span of the whole of the first fifty years since the Rising of 1916, cynicism is surely without justification. After all, when Cavour said, at the time of the Risorgimento, 'If we did for ourselves what we do for our country we would be arrant scoundrels' – a phrase delightful to all those people, in Italy as well as Ireland, two highly cynical countries, who like to think that every politician is a dishonest rogue – his acid piece of auto-criticism may have wounded his fellow politicians but it assassinated his electors. No politician represents only himself. In representing millions he can do nothing and say nothing that is not contingent on the aggregate wishes of those millions. Do I hear the reader growling the word, Leadership? One need do no more than flick an eye at the contemporary political scene anywhere in the world to see how often leadership is hamstrung by the very people who most eloquently ask for it. Every politician has to live by a dual morality – one code for his private behaviour, another for his public behaviour – imposed on him by those of us who disingenuously think him more disingenuous than ourselves.

This dual morality is the ultimate justification of that modern phenomenon, Protest. Without outspoken, sometimes even violent protest, democracy stagnates. It can only operate vigorously where there is a constant seesaw between the oracular in politics and the outspoken in protest. So, it has been said of the oracle of Delphos, without whose advice no new laws were enacted, no new colonies founded by Greece, that what it was in practice was not a divine voice but a thoroughly human information bureau operating through a network of astute intelligence agents spread throughout the country. Every politician may like to think himself his own Oracle – Mr de Valera once said that when he wanted to know what Ireland wanted he looked into his own heart – but he knows well that his essential information comes from the fields, the streets and those few uncommitted thinkers whose vocation it is to interpret the grumbling murmurs of the pavements and the ominous silences of the ploughlands. It is not surprising if the politician often fails to hear these protesting noises, or if he heeds them, that he should ask, impatiently 'What exactly do they want?' In fact 'they' rarely do know. Programmatically they must not know! Their interest is not so much to get something new done as to get something old undone by thrashing it out to its roots all over again. The role of all protesters is not to answer questions but to ask them, uncomfortably and persistently.

We have had our protesters, sometimes violent, rarely articulate or creative, but they have been all too few. We have not learned the lesson Franklin Delano Roosevelt learned from the great Depression in time to utter it on the eve of the War against the dictators:

If by democratic methóds people get a strong enough government to protect them from fear and starvation, their democracy succeeds; if they do not, they grow impatient. The only sure bulwark of continuing liberty is a government strong enough to protect the interests of the people, *and a people strong enough and well informed enough to maintain its control over the government.*

To which one might add another observation, learned also from a lifetime of politics, by Charles Evan Hughes, twice Governor of New York, Chief Justice of the Supreme Court and Secretary of State under two Presidents:

The greater the importance of safeguarding the community from incitements by force and violence, the more imperative the need to preserve inviolate the constitutional rights of free speech, free press and free assembly in order to maintain the opportunity of political discussion, to the end that government may be responsible to the will of the people, and that changes, if desired, may be obtained by peaceful means. Therein lies the security of the Republic, the very foundation of constitutional government.

There need have been no stagnation, no IRA, no censorship, if this wisdom had inspired Ireland from 1922 on. That it did not is evident alone in the memory of those thirty chilling years and more of government censorship during which over ten thousand authors were banned; including almost every Irish writer of note, under the pretence that they were indecent but actually (the case of Brendan Behan's memoirs is in point) to silence every frank attempt to delineate the society in which he lived.* If our politicians had been more intelligent, if Delphos

---

* The Censorship started in 1929 under the first Free State government and was continued forcefully throughout the de Valera régime. It is one of the signs of the new wind of change that it was modified in 1967 to such

had really wanted to smell the winds of change, foresee and prepare for the future which is now our present, they would from the very beginning have initiated a crash programme of secularized education on strictly modern lines, subsidized periodicals and publishing wholesale – not merely to invite but to encourage in every man an intelligent public opinion – lavishly subsidized the arts, and above all resolutely insisted on the separation of the newborn state from our old conservative peasant church whose dead hand has lain so heavily on every least movement of progressive thought that when one government proposed a most modest scheme of socialized medicine for mothers and children the assembled bishops of Ireland crushed it by *ukase*.* Because none of those things was done, our sails sagged for a generation; we lived under the hypnosis of the past, our timidities about the future, our excessive reverence for old traditions, our endemic fear of new ways, of new thinking, the opiate of that absurd historical myth, and, the horror of the feeling of solitude that comes on every man who dares push out his boat from the security of his old, cosy, familiar harbour into unknown seas.

It was not until about 1959 that, for good or ill all this began to change and a new wind began to blow over Ireland. In that

effect that all authors banned up to ten years before that date were unbanned, and that no future book may now be banned for more than ten years. The horrid thing is evidently on its way out. Stupid things are still done under the Act, but, in the main, only the cheapest stuff, mostly gaudy American pulp paperbacks, are now banned.

*In a letter to the then Minister for Health, Dr Noel Browne, the secretary to the hierarchy outlined its reasons for opposing the scheme. Parts of it are most revealing, e.g.:

'[In the bishops' opinion] the powers taken by the State in the proposed Mother and Child Health Service are in direct opposition to the rights of the family and the individual, and are liable to very great abuse. . . . If adopted in law they would constitute a ready-made instrument for future totalitarian aggression. The right [*sic*] to provide for the health of children belongs to parents, not to the State.' On sex teaching: 'We regard with the greatest apprehension the proposal to give to local medical officers the right to give instructions to Catholic girls and women in this sphere of conduct. . . . We have no guarantee that State officials will respect Catholic principles in regard to those matters.'

This warm trust of the Bishops in their own flock was very kindly received on all sides.

year Mr de Valera retired from active politics and was succeeded by a very different type of man, Mr Sean Lemass.

At this point, since I am obviously not drawn to Mr de Valera as a politician – as a man he has great personal charm and is, to use a suitably old-fashioned word, a gentleman to his fingertips – it is only fair to quote from the work of somebody who finds him more *simpatico*. The following comes from that immeasurably useful volume, *Ireland Since the Rising*, by T. P. Coogan*:

The day de Valera took over power (in 1932) most of his followers carried revolvers in their pockets as they took their seats with him ... [The revolver is, of course, our great psychological sexual symbol of the Past]... He left it some thirty years later, probably to go down in history as an even greater figure than Parnell. He had used every possible manoeuvre during his career on the national stage: a career longer than Franco's, Salazar's or Stalin's, and unlike theirs devoted to democracy. Few statesmen of his century could claim to have pursued their aims with more tenacity, skill and simplicity. After his withdrawal from parliamentary politics, and despite the fact that the country was now visibly beginning to lift itself from the long stagnation, Fianna Fail's majority fell ...

I cannot refrain from adding that I think that the clue to Mr de Valera's success on the hustings is that he was always – a not uncharacteristic Irish blend – a combination of realism, sentimentality and ruthlessness, in which each was always corrupting the other. All idealists are ruthless. Every politician has his sentimental streak. Even Stalin had a daughter; Hitler loved his dog; Napoleon wept over the poems of Ossian. When a politician becomes sentimental then is the time for all good men to reach for the ballot-paper.†

Mr Sean Lemass was a frank modernizer who had the good fortune to inherit from a previous government (the 1955–7 coalition under Mr John Costello) a decision of its Minister for

---

*London, 1966, p. 105.

† It may also be remarked that Mr Coogan dates the end of (his phrase) 'the long stagnation' to an election in 1957 'which showed that in their desperation for change people were even prepared to vote for violence'. His reference then is to the first appearance of the IRA who won four seats at that election, but, true to old tradition, still refused, alas, to enter the Dáil and, so once more disappeared into the shadows.

Finance, Mr Gerard Sweetman, which was to have a profound effect on Irish economic affairs: the appointment as Secretary to the Department of Finance of a professional economist (and a later convert to planning) named T. K. Whitaker. Even before Lemass took office Whitaker's ideas about the nature of the society we ought to be creating and the manner in which it might be created had already begun to influence the economy. Under Lemass, in 1958, a unique publication, *Economic Development*, drawn up by Whitaker and his associates, officially published but not officially approved by the Government, initiated the First Programme for Economic Expansion, followed in 1963 by the Second Programme, to cover the period to 1970. The interested reader studying these programmes should put beside them the policy document of the opposition party, *The Just Society*, and consult further Chapters 5 and 7 of Mr Coogan's book (op. cit.) for some of the details and general implications of Whitaker's proposals. It must also be observed that in 1968 the Second Programme for Irish Economic Planning had to be officially dropped because it had meanwhile become clear that its assumptions had been unrealistic, especially in relation to agriculture whose stagnation in output had been entirely unforeseen.

Briefly, what began to happen after 1958 was an intensive drive – aimed at increasing exports and preparing for Common Market conditions – to rationalize Irish economics inside a comprehensive interlocked plan blending private enterprise and state-sponsored, state-encouraged and state-financed industries. Some of these latter had always been with us, but a considerable extra stress was now placed on all three. For example, foreign capital willing to open factories for exports was offered such incentives as exemption from income tax, and corporation tax on profits for the first ten years. At times large grants, up to two thirds or more of the cost of building installations, were also available for manufacturers for export. As a result, 'between 1955 and 1964,' Coogan has calculated, '200 new industrial enterprises were set up, providing jobs for some 26,000 people and representing an injection of £48 million in new capital'. Not that all these enterprises succeeded; there have been some spectacular failures, such as the loss of £1½ million in one industry alone, the proposed light aircraft factory of the French firm Potez which was not, after all, in a position to produce a single aircraft. The planners, however, maintain that not only are such losses part of the game – as, indeed, anybody who has watched the progress of similar schemes elsewhere, such as in southern Italy, must agree – but that they have been fewer than had been anticipated, and even less than their plans could carry. As to the source of all the stimulating money this injected, shot by shot, into our economy one has only to ask the taxpayer and the investor; noting, especially, that between 1960 and 1968 the net capital liabilities of the state increased from £215 million to £434 million.*

As to the long-term soundness of any economy energized in this way nobody can speak infallibly : unpredictable factors are always liable to upset such schemes and prove once again that there are no scientific constants in economics. Certainly no traditional economist who clings to the gospel that a state ought to balance its books, if not year by year, at least every five years, observing that since 1929, with the exception of one statistic (that for 1944). Ireland consistently imported far more than it exported, could only gravely shake his head. On the other hand the planner, with his eye less on present trade deficits than on the future for which he was planning – or on which, the traditionalist would sourly say, he was gambling – would as emphatically nod his head, and get on with the job. In all such circumstances the citizen who, whatever happens, has to pay *his* debts on the nail could only bow his head and hope for the best.

The Irish electorate of the fifties had asked for change and they got it. They had wanted modernization and found it about them in a flood. If they were weary of the Past they should, by 1965, have been weary no more; it was on its way out, for, though lip service might still be paid to it, countless contemporary influences were fast abrading its pristine power – the lure of more money, the growth of material incentives, the desire for more possessions, a rapidly rising standard of living

* Between 1970 and 1979 the National Debt increased from £1,000 million to £6,000 million, and foreign debt rose from £70 million to a staggering £1,320 million.

measured always, not unnaturally, by close contacts with British and other ways of life, through radio, television, the cinema and the press, through foreign travel, the immense development of tourism as one of our major industries, even through the ecumenical tide of thought. Time was when common words on every lip in every Irish pub were Partition, The Civil War, The Republic, The Gun. The vocabulary of the mid-fifties and sixties was very different – The Common Market, Planning, Growth Rates, Strikes, Jobs, Educational Opportunities, or why this factory failed or that one flourished, and if some still raised apprehensive questions about our William Tells nobody any longer seemed to care a damn about Oliver Cromwell or the Black and Tans. Age was, no doubt, a relevant factor. In 1968 Mr de Valera was eighty-six and Mrs de Valera had turned ninety. In 1968 the leader of the party Mr de Valera had once led, Mr Jack Lynch, was fifty. Unborn in 1916, a child of four when the Free State was founded, he had never seen a Black and Tan and could only know of the old frugal, patriarchal Ireland by tradition. But nobody in Ireland under fifty, apart from novelists and historians, now cares a damn about the nineteenth century. One afternoon in 1967 an inquiring television reporter stood with a microphone and camera in O'Connell Street, pointed to the statue of Smith O'Brien, the once revered leader of the Young Ireland Party, sentenced to death in 1848, and asked a dozen passers-by, 'Who is he?' Nobody knew.

Whatever happens to our economy in time, our central question will long remain. Did that final swing to modernization bring Ireland even one Whitaker nearer to the realization of the old 1916 Republican vision of life? I believe that it did, by at least a generation, if only because its concentration on the necessity for economic development, at almost any cost, at least forced us all to realize that an impoverished Republican is a contradiction in terms; and that Lenin was right in his famous dogma that all political institutions are no more than a superstructure resting on economic foundations.

We could, nevertheless, also see, as those new programmes got under way, that the soundest economic foundations can also support the most unattractive superstructure, and that the words 'political institutions' are meaningless as long as they remain undefined by the human shape of life that they are supposed to embody. It became clear to us in the sixties that if our Nationalism was merely phase one, modernization could only be phase two overlapping its predecessor like the stones in a corbel roof. We had only to look about us at the present and the past of Britain, France or the United States to observe that in none of them has any political institution ever of itself pre-empted poverty, racism, selfish privilege, imperialism, ghettoes for Negroes, Jews, Puerto Ricans, West Indians, or under-privileged workers – all summed up as the evil fruits of that horrid thing that, in the sixties, plenty of Irishmen were still grimly calling Mammonism.

They could smell it in the dust of the reckless demolition of some of Dublin's finest old buildings to make room for new and mostly hideous commercial offices that could just as well and more conveniently have been built outside the city's handsome centre; they could see it in the depopulation of the countryside; more deeply in many examples of inequality of opportunity for the mass of the people. To quote but one such example: in 1968 only between 3 per cent and 4 per cent of the children of our farmers were attending our universities, as compared with 37 per cent from the higher professional groups, and only 2 per cent from the skilled workers' group. In the west, at University College, Galway, 1 per cent of the students were the children of labourers; in the east, at Trinity College, Dublin, this group was completely unrepresented – the main reason for this loss of potential ability being that the mass of our young people were not even completing their secondary education. In short it would seem that modernization was going hand in hand with selfish privilege.*

If, by now, the reader has not begun to see why all these prob-lems – even racism and imperialism, through our involvement in international politics – are problems that we still have to solve, and will for a long time yet go on trying to solve, I have failed dismally to make clear that the outstanding thing about

*Figures taken from 'A Study of the Social Background of Students in the Irish Universities', read to the Statistical and Social Inquiry Society, at the Royal Irish Academy, by Monica Nevin, Department of Psychology, University College, Dublin, in 1968.

the development of a national intellect is the amazing slowness, difficulty and complexity of what we once thought of as a simple process. The new Ireland is still learning this old lesson the hard way, like a brilliant but arrogant boy whose very brilliance acts as a dam against experience, so that he learns everything quickly — except experience. Our Nationalism has for far too long been our Egoism. It was our lovely, shining youth. Like all the appurtenances of youth it was lovely in its day. After its day passed to attempt to wear it was a form of 'Death in Venice', a middle-aged man raddling his cheeks to keep his youthful glow in times of plague. Ireland has clung to her youth, indeed to her childhood, longer and more tenaciously than any other country in Europe, resisting Change, Alteration, Reconstruction to the very last.

Nationalism, according to Marx, withers away when the national ego is satisfied. (Any Irishman, looking at Britain and the British Empire in the nineteenth century could only remark, with a certain dryness, that it certainly withers very nicely into Imperialism.) Any Irishman, looking about him in Ireland even as recently as thirty years ago, could only have remarked wearily that Nationalism is an appetite that grows by what it feeds on. Today I see some signs of a withering of our outmoded Nationalism. If it is even still with us in large patches I record with satisfaction that it has there bloated into xenophobia and chauvinism. I say 'with satisfaction' because the great difference between a normal patriotism and a dropsical chauvinism is not so much that the one is healthy and the other is a disease as that the one is common property and the other is private property; by which I mean that I do not believe that patriotism is the last refuge of a scoundrel, but I do believe that chauvinism is. And although I have never studied the life of the original Sergeant Chauvin, who caused himself to be lowered into the grave by knotted tricolours, I should be greatly surprised if he did not also climb in the world as many of our modern entrepreneurs have done under cover of the flag.

It has taken a long time for the groups to take clear shape. As they do so — liberals, socialists, acquisitive middle classes, bureaucrats, chauvinists, professional pietists, professional peasants (the Good Old Days men), the frank and brutal racketeers, the con-men, the speculators, the men with a social conscience and the men with none – the real human tensions at last become intelligible and recognizable, and the stage is set for phase three, which will be the seeming slowest of all because it will never end: the creation of a way of life, spiritually, bodily and above all intellectually expressive of the Irish nature: a pattern of living equally satisfying what a recent critic of Claude Lévi-Strauss has called man's 'reasoned nostalgia for a primitive integrity now lost, and a reasoned optimism that some substitute for it may be produced by taking the right kind of thought'.

Thought? History is not a tale told by the fireside. It is an ever-developing process, and all its events not so much events as thoughts hammered into mortal heads. I have quoted the late R. G. Collingwood for my epigraph to this book: 'History proper is the history of thought: there are no mere events in history.' He goes on to explain that all seeming historical events are in practice actions that express some intention, or purpose of their agents, and that the historian's job is to identify the thought behind each act, and also, surely, to measure the thought's worth or worthlessness? For, as he says, many seeming actions, or *actiones* are really merely *passiones*, or things that men just put up with or endure. I fear that for Ireland much of our history is made up of endurances, so that for us moderns to make any meaningful historical synthesis out of our past, to abstract the basic lessons from our experience, is particularly difficult. However, we have achieved one lesson. If, in the long view of history we Irish have thus far learned little, and that slowly, from our actions and our passions, we have at least begun to learn how to learn. We will, painfully, learn more.

How beautiful, as Chekhov used to say of his Russia, life in Ireland will be in two hundred years' time!

APPENDIX

In saying (page 148) that living conditions and a living culture are not the same thing I do not wish to be understood as saying that there is no relationship between them. There obviously is, but it is not always a fruitful relationship. People do not automatically become more cultured by becoming more rich; and though it has in the past happened that way after many generations, modern methods of taxation go far to interrupt this traditional process of transmission. Your modern Texan oil millionaire, possibly descended from cowboy stock (and, by the way, the cowboy had his own fine kind of indigenous culture) may demonstrate his secret reverence for the culture he missed on the way by buying Matisses and Picassos and sending his son to Harvard; but he cannot be sure that his grandson may not revert to type. A self-made Boston millionaire may send his son to Harvard and even help him to become President of the United States. Yet some Boston brahmin has said, most unkindly, of the Kennedys as a family, that they came too late to be plain green and too soon to be true blue. The relationship between living conditions and a living culture is a very complex matter, as I may be able to demonstrate by reference to two long-pedigreed efforts to improve living conditions in Ireland.

In our early, propagandist Sinn Fein days and later, after the Rising of 1916, patriotic Irishmen did develop, chiefly in their political weekly papers, many imaginative schemes to improve living conditions by harnessing the rivers, mining the earth, planting the barren mountains and so on; and we have, since then, duly harnessed, mined and planted, sometimes successfully and sometimes not.

Let us take electricity and mining and see what has actually happened. It is gratifying to be able to record that, thanks to the Shannon and other hydro-electric schemes, the use of electricity has now become widespread in rural as well as urban Ireland and it has been of great benefit to both. It is also gratifying to note that Irish domestic consumers of electricity pay less than their counterparts in Britain and Northern Ireland (January, 1980). So, a domestic consumer in London, using 3,300 units a year, pays 4.039 new pence per unit; in Bristol, 3.901 pence per unit; in Belfast, 4.622 pence per unit; in Liverpool, 3.892 pence per unit; in Birmingham, 3.765 pence per unit, whereas in Dublin and other urban areas he pays 3.427 pence per unit and outside Dublin, in rural areas, 3.645 pence per unit. In Edinburgh, which still largely generates power by water, the consumer pays only 3.325 pence per unit. In all cases it is assumed, as in the case of London, that the average domestic consumer uses 3,300 units a year.

The prime cost of the capitalization of these Irish electrical schemes is, of course, another matter and introduces us to an interesting social problem that has over the years developed inside this industry. Some of our electricity is generated from peat rather than from water power and imported oil, and this is not strictly economic. Is it going too far to say, as some critics have forcibly said, that peat-made electricity is not an industry at all but a disguised dole invented solely to give employment in remote rural areas? (It provides employment for some 4,000 people.) The answer is complex, and as follows:

In the 1960s the Irish peat production authority, a state enterprise called Bord na Mona, meaning the Turf Board, had been instructed to sell its peat to the Electricity Supply Board at a price below the cost of production. Otherwise the price of electricity would have soared. At the same time, Bord na Mona has also been required to pay interest at fixed rates on all capital advances received from the Exchequer, as well as to begin the repayment of the prime capital as soon as the bogs in which the capital was invested have been developed and come into production. (All of Bord na Mona's state-advanced capital is, in any case, repayable on a twenty-five years basis – the estimated life of a peat-bog.) Between 1946 and 1969 Bord na Mona repaid nearly £4 million of the capital thus advanced to it by the state, as well as interest amounting to nearly £8½ million. Between 1965 and 1970, however, it failed to meet its financial obligations, mainly because of two consecutive years of bad weather and, consequently, of bad harvests, combined with the fact that peat still had to be sold to the E.S.B. below cost. We return, then, to our criticism that those early optimistic Sinn Fein dreams of exploiting the earth (e.g. for coal and peat) and harnessing the rivers (e.g. for electric power) can succeed only by leaning on one another and/or on the subsidizing tax-payer, and that peat production as we know it is not a strictly economic industry but a form of social service. Furthermore, the O.P.E.C. crisis of 1973 has completely changed the picture. Sinn Fein could not have foreseen such complexities.

The main problem for the Turf Board is now not the old one of its low price to the E.S.B. but (a) that the public demand has greatly increased, and (b) that the peat bogs are approaching the point of exhaustion.

The following table reveals how dependent the E.S.B. has become on imported oil over the five years since the spring of 1974:

Sources of Electricity Generated in the Republic *

	Year ended March 1974	Year ended March 1979
Oil	64%	73%
Peat	25%	19%
Hydro	10%	7%
Coal	1%	1%

This brings us to mining. In 1970, rather tardily in the history of the Republic (none of whose budding industrialists seem to have read Sir Robert Kane's great book *The Industrial Resources of Ireland*), Rio Tinto, one of the world's largest mining companies, began prospecting near Navan, some twenty-nine miles from Dublin. The main result was that, when Rio Tinto withdrew, a few chaps, feeling that there *must* be something in the area, started what is now patriotically known as Tara Mines and discovered about 77 million tons of lead–zinc deposits. Unluckily, some more chaps with a similar idea acquired adjacent land above these deposits; an area that became known as Bula Mines. The upshot to date of the resultant legal battle is that Tara won,

* I am indebted to Professor Patrick Lynch, Department of Economics, University College, Dublin, for these interesting figures.

the government paying Bula £9.25 million for a 24 per cent investment therein, receiving in addition a gift of a further 25 per cent investment, leaving the government owning 51 per cent of the shares in Bula. However, nothing has so far (early 1980) got under way, due to objections of the local authorities and the objections of environmentalists to opencast mining. Meanwhile Tara has borrowed £70 million and given the government a 25 per cent share in its property. Elsewhere it appears that minor discoveries of barytes have been modestly successful, and that some initial exploration for uranium took place in 1979. In general, mineral development in Ireland is not viewed with the optimism of three-quarters of a century ago.

Here, then, are two schemes both aimed at improving living conditions in the Irish Republic, both concerned with what nowadays is called Energy. As has been said above, the now widespread use of electrical energy has done much to improve living conditions in rural as well as urban Ireland. What of the general effect on culture? If we take the word culture in its larger, that is in its social, sense, electrical energy has quite transformed the character of rural life. It has helped to reduce the drudgery of farm life, fostered a greater use of machinery by the men, offered their wives such basic benefits as a constant supply of indoor hot water, helped to make even the most modest cottage bright as well as warm, helped to keep young people on the land, and profitably, in every sense, encouraged tourists to venture more off the beaten track.

If, however, we take the word culture in its more specialized sense of enlightenment and refinement (words which should always carry inverted commas) and of preserving traditional ways and values, the question becomes imponderable. One may, for instance, find it difficult to answer such a question as whether it is profitable, in this sense of the word culture, to 'keep the young on the land' if 'the land' means wide, rather bleak and perforce under-populated peat bogs whose product is already beginning to disappear. One may have to consider objectively whether any traditional culture can long withstand the manifold effects of industrialization, with the example of the industrialized regions of South Wales and Scotland in mind or, indeed, modern invasions anywhere such as air travel, the telephone, television, radio, discos, dance-halls and the Press. It must be disturbing for traditionalists to observe that J. M. Synge's *The Playboy of the Western World* island of Aran now has an airstrip, television, electric power, radio, canned food and telephones. As for mining, nothing that one has read or heard about any kind of mining, for coal, diamonds, salt or metals, in any part of the world, leads one to think highly of its cultural effects on those engaged in it. At best it is a wide-open question whether they are not generally harmful effects. My point is that whether they are or not this is precisely the kind of question never faced by those who concentrate on improving material subsistence conditions to the exclusion of the larger and deeper cultural considerations that lie behind them.

MORE ABOUT PENGUINS, PELICANS
AND PUFFINS

For further information about books available from Penguins please write to Dept EP, Penguin Books Ltd, Harmondsworth, Middlesex UB7 0DA.

In the U.S.A.: For a complete list of books available from Penguins in the United States write to Dept DG, Penguin Books, 299 Murray Hill Parkway, East Rutherford, New Jersey 07073.

In Canada: For a complete list of books available from Penguins in Canada write to Penguin Books Canada Ltd, 2801 John Street, Markham, Ontario L3R 1B4.

In Australia: For a complete list of books available from Penguins in Australia write to the Marketing Department, Penguin Books Australia Ltd, P.O. Box 257, Ringwood, Victoria 3134.

In New Zealand: For a complete list of books available from Penguins in New Zealand write to the Marketing Department, Penguin Books (N.Z.) Ltd, P.O. Box 4019, Auckland 10.

In India: For a complete list of books available from Penguins in India write to Penguin Overseas Ltd, 706 Eros Apartments, 56 Nehru Place, New Delhi 110019.